**Genette: Where is She No**

One hot Saturday, thirteen year-old Genette Tate took her bicycle out of the garden shed and set off on a weekend paper round.

Hours later, two of her friends found her bicycle lying abandoned at the side of a quiet country lane.

Despite a massive police operation and intense media publicity, John Tate is still no nearer to knowing his daughter's fate.

*Genette: Where is She Now?* tells the story of John Tate's ordeal, and how he discovered a new faith and hope in his darkest moments.

But it is more than one man's story. Out of this tragedy, the organization *International Find a Child* was born, dedicated to help the growing number of parents whose children vanish each year.

*To Genette*

# Genette

## WHERE IS SHE NOW?

## John Tate

A LION PAPERBACK
Tring · Belleville · Sydney

Copyright © 1985 Lion Publishing

Published by
**Lion Publishing plc**
Icknield Way, Tring, Herts, England
ISBN 0 85648 901 8
**Lion Publishing Corporation**
10885 Textile Road, Belleville, Michigan 48111, USA
ISBN 0 85648 901 8
**Albatross Books**
PO Box 320, Sutherland, NSW 2232, Australia
ISBN 0 86760 623 1

**British Library Cataloguing in Publication Data**

Tate, John
  Genette: Where is She Now?
  1. Missing persons—Great Britain—Case
  studies  2. Children—Great Britain—Case
  studies
  I. Title
  362.7′044    HQ792.G7
  ISBN 0-85648-901-8

First edition 1985
Printed by Cox & Wyman Ltd, Reading

Song lyrics on page 109
© Restoration Music 1983
and used by permission.

# Contents

1 Genette Disappears 7
2 One Week Later 25
3 Rewards and Red Herrings 43
4 Meeting the Press 51
5 A Christmas Alone 61
6 Turning the Corner 73
7 A Narrow Escape 85
8 New Beginnings 93
9 Did this Man Kill Genette? 99
10 The Wheels Begin to Turn 107
11 Where Have All the Children Gone? 119
12 Runaways and Hideaways 127
13 The Unsolved Disappearances 145
14 How Can We Help? 151
   Useful Addresses 160

# 1
# Genette Disappears

On Saturday 19 August 1978, thirteen year-old Genette Tate took her bicycle out of the garden shed and set off on a weekend paper round in the tranquil village of Aylesbeare, Devon.

Hours later, two of her friends found her bicycle lying abandoned at the side of a quiet country lane, with copies of the newspaper spilling out of the carrier. Of Genette, the girl with a smile that lit up her whole face, there was no sign.

Calling her name, Genette's friends became anxious. Where had she disappeared to? But there was no answer. Puzzled, they picked up the bicycle and the newspapers and left the scene to tell Mr and Mrs Tate.

Seven years later we are no closer to knowing Genette's fate than we were on that hot summer's day when she vanished.

Genette's disappearance triggered off a massive police operation, intense media coverage, and a whole train of events that would affect far more people than anyone involved could ever have foreseen.


Our daughter Genette Louise Tate was a fun-loving schoolgirl, much loved, and much cared for. She had been born one spring day in 1965 — and she immediately made her presence felt. For the first three months of her life, like many young babies, she suffered from colic, and her crying caused us all kinds of anxieties and a great many sleepless nights. It may only have been a three-month spell, but at the time it seemed more like three years.

Little brown-eyed Genette was talking at nine months, walking at eighteen months and, to our great relief, grew a head of curls when she was two years old. What a relief — our daughter was not going to be bald after all!

Her natural inquisitiveness and desire to learn without appearing to be a know-it-all made her enthusiastic in school and popular with children of her own age. I can still remember her serious expression at the tender age of two, as she solemnly studied the writhings of a worm in our garden. Her brown eyes were wide as she watched the creature burrow its way earthwards.

Genette started school when she was five and loved every minute of it. Right from the early days she showed a real aptitude for mental arithmetic and shone in French and English lessons. As she grew older she began to write poetry — something that became one of her favourite hobbies. Genette's last school report, in the early summer of 1978, was a joy to read and we were very proud of our young daughter. She was a pupil at Exmouth comprehensive school, then the largest in the country.

Like a hundred-and-one other young girls, Genette spoke of taking up nursing as a career — when she wasn't dreaming of joining the police force. She was a little worried that she'd never be quite tall enough to become a police woman, and for a while began to think about becoming a vet. That is, until she watched a TV series that showed the work of a country vet in graphic detail! After that she changed her mind most definitely.

All in all, she was a normal teenager.

On that morning in August 1978 — that last morning — I left the house at 7.30 a.m. with my wife Violet (Genette's step-mother) to take her to work at the hospital in Exeter. Then I drove to the doctor's surgery in nearby Woodbury to see about my sore throat. I was soon back home preparing breakfast for Genette and her step-sister Tania. Breakfast included fried bread — not one of Genette's favourites.

The girls were chattering excitedly. Tania was about to spend a fortnight's holiday with her father in Cornwall, and I could hear the pair of them giggling and laughing in anticipation. It was just like a hot August day should be.

After breakfast had been eaten and the cleaning up was completed, Tania packed the last-minute odds and ends that always get left out of the suitcase. Genette took her much-loved puzzle books into the garden, and sat out in the sun. I tried to persuade her to come with us to see Tania off at the bus station, and to pick up Violet. We could do her paper round later in the car, I suggested. But Genette had arranged to do the round with Tony Hammond, her boyfriend, so she turned down the offer. (We found out later that Genette and Tony failed to meet up as arranged.)

At almost half past twelve, Tania, her boyfriend David and I said goodbye to Genette and set off to collect Tania's young friend Julie. On our way to the bus station we went into Exeter to collect Violet from the hospital. The roads were crowded with holiday-makers, and the coach station was a mass of bodies rushing like disturbed ants as people tried to track down the coach that would take them away from it all.

Eventually we squeezed Tania and Julie onto a fast-filling coach, and although we were sure it was the right one, we waited until 3.10 for the laden coach to leave so that we could wave goodbye. Watching the coach manoeuvre its way out of the station, my mind went to Genette. I remember thinking that she would be half-way through her paper round by now, cycling through green leafy roads, away from all the smog, muck and grime of the city.

Then another picture came to mind, and I could almost feel the sand between my toes on Cornwall's Vault Beach, where we once lived. It was to be an oft-returning memory of stillness and peace in the days to come.

Violet and I, assured that Tania and her friend were safely despatched, made our way home in a leisurely fashion, stopping for an ice cream to make the heat more bearable. We talked about baking hot beaches, holidays and relaxation.

Pulling up outside Barton Farm Cottage, we little realized what lay in wait for us. The most important thing on our minds was how long it would take us to brew up a pot of life-saving tea. Violet got out to put the kettle on while I drove the car into the farmyard to park.

It was then that the long, long nightmare began. Violet came rushing up to me, her face anxious and worried. She was pushing Genette's bicycle and behind her was Tracey, one of Genette's friends. Tracey was trying to tell us that Genette was nowhere to be found. And so the clouds of worry shut out that warm August sun, and all that Violet, Tracey and I could think of was *where* was Genette?

We went straight away to Within Lane, where Genette's bike had been found, and we walked up and down, up and down, up and down, calling her name and half expecting to hear her cheery voice and see her smile at any moment. We knocked on the doors of all the houses we passed, urgently asking if Genette had been there. The village lads willingly set to and began scrambling about local fields and hedges. Where *was* she?

It seemed as though an eternity had passed before Violet said that we must go to the police. We were quite distraught as we made our way home — perhaps Genette had arrived back while all the fuss was at its height and was wondering if she was going to have to get her own tea. But the house was empty and silent.

Heavy-hearted, we went to see the village policeman, Constable Laws. He knew Genette, of course, but we still had to give him a description, paying special attention to what she had been wearing. What *had* she been wearing? For a moment I couldn't think. But then it all came back — a white cotton top with a high rounded neckline, with the name 'Genette' embroidered in red across the left shoulder; a pair of brown trousers, and white pumps. The description, issued by the police later that day, added the information that thirteen year-old Ginny was '5ft tall, with short brown hair and brown eyes, is suntanned and looks her age'.

After seeing the constable, we telephoned Exeter police headquarters. 'Go home and wait,' they told us.

Back home, through the windows, we could see uniformed policemen searching with dogs. Searching for our Genette. It didn't seem real somehow. It was all a bad dream and any minute Genette was going to come running into my arms, crying 'daddy'.

The phone rang — the police again. But no Genette.

From the windows we could see across the fields, to where Genette's bicycle had been found. Even as we stared, mesmerized at that spot, the first contingent of policemen arrived on the doorstep, full of questions. They searched her room, her drawers and cupboards, asked what she was wearing, who were her friends, was she happy, had she had an argument, had she run away before, where might she go to hide. It just didn't seem right. Why would Genette run away from us? We were so sure she hadn't.

The day dragged on interminably. Weary and fearful, the sound of a helicopter flying low over the village revived our flagging hopes. We all rushed outside. Surely this would be the way to find Genette and bring her back to us. It made a warm tingle run up my spine, to think that British justice could act so quickly. No other country, I thought proudly, could boast such care and speed and efficiency.

Slowly the harsh sunlight gave way to evening's softer shadows, and as dark's cool fingers crept stealthily across the village, a gentle, sweet rain began to fall. My vivid imagination pictured Genette caught in the shower.

I imagined her struggling up out of a ditch or field staggering and dazed and damp. So I rushed out and drove around and around, through all the lanes and roads, looking for that familiar figure. After one of the circuits I found myself back in the village. There I met a group of people still searching in the damp darkness with only two torches between them. 'Please God, let the rain stop!' my anguished self cried out.

Much as I hated to admit it, I and the other searchers had to accept that it was pointless to continue in the darkness.

'Go home and sleep,' said kindly villagers. Sleep? How could there be sleep until Genette had been found?

But at 3.30 a.m. we went home to bed nevertheless and lay there, unable to sleep, until 5.00 a.m. Then we were up and out in the lanes again. We searched this part of the common, then that. We walked up the lanes and down the paths, stared into ditches and over hedges. We even went to the nearby M5 Exeter Services, where many tired holidaymakers took overnight rest on their long holiday treks, and peered into every parked car. We found nothing, absolutely nothing. Not one single clue to suggest where Genette had gone.

So many possibilities preyed on our minds: she had been kidnapped, raped, or murdered, or she'd fallen off her bike and was wandering around somewhere with amnesia. Surely none of these things could have happened to our lovely little girl?

The hours of searching proved fruitless and we realized that we had gone without food for nearly twenty-four hours. So we went home to eat. The food seemed to taste like cardboard but we felt we ought to eat something to keep our strength up.

An organized search party of villagers and police began a systematic combing of the area. Because I suffered from a mild form of muscular dystrophy, which made continuous exercise difficult, I agreed to stay by the phone, while Violet joined in the search.

So the first of what was to be many searches began, and I sat by that phone desperately hoping. During the morning, Sheila, Genette's mother, rang to say that she was coming over. Genette had been four-and-a-half when her mother and I parted, but we had allowed the past to be forgotten and had become friends of sorts for the sake of Genette. Suddenly, as I was talking to Sheila, I was flooded by a new realization of what was happening and I cried and cried. I was overwhelmed with feelings of inadequacy as I realized that my beloved daughter could be absolutely anywhere. Even with so many people helping us to look, the task of finding Genette seemed enormous.

The police returned to the house in search of more detailed statements. They asked questions like there was no tomorrow. My head was buzzing, but I desperately wanted to help. I kept wondering if somewhere, somehow, I had the key to Genette's disappearance. If I had, I desperately wanted to find it.

Friends of the family arrived at the house offering comfort and a friendly presence. High above in the azure summer sky a helicopter resumed its sweeps over the Aylesbeare countryside.

As the minutes dragged on into hours, I became acutely aware of the impotency in waiting. Waiting for news, for a clue, for anything that might advance the search. The hours began to blur and blend together — we felt as though we were in a daze.

By mid-afternoon, the police had made hundreds of copies of Genette's school photo — and we took a few handfuls and headed up onto Woodbury Common. There we started searching for Genette, and asked the many people enjoying the peace of a Sunday afternoon's sunshine if they had seen her.

We walked across the common, calling her name as we went, in the hope that she might be somewhere amongst the deep bracken that covered the lovely area with its August greenery. Beautiful as it was, the common began to take on a different meaning for us, and we wished we had a Land Rover so that we could see over the top of the tall, tangled undergrowth. The task was just impossible for a small family group.

Eventually we went home to try to get one of the radio stations to appeal for people to be on the lookout for Genette.

Sunday rolled onwards into Monday, and the days

seemed unimportant. Waiting seemed so intolerable. By Monday, Genette was still missing and the local search attracted nationwide press interest. Someone else's heartbreak became bread and butter for some, a source of detached interest for others.

The first TV interviews were awesome enough, with lights, cameras, wires and people everywhere, but the press conference that followed seemed even worse. We were quite frightened of the reporters at first, but our desire to do anything that might help us find our daughter, coupled with the support of the police, helped us to cope.

We did two interviews for television. The first was a bit of a blur as we just felt stunned. The second was a horrifying experience, with our fears and emotions overcoming us. I suppose we were realizing again the shock of it all.

Then, later in the day, when the interviews were broadcast on the news, it felt so strange. There we were, just ordinary people, appearing on the television, appealing for help in tracing our missing daughter. My heart still misses a beat even today when that much-used photograph appears on the screen with those words, 'Genette Tate'.

But on that first occasion it was as though an icy cold gust of wind had caught me unawares. I stood there frozen to the spot wondering whether or not I should cry.

After that came more searching. Dozens of pairs of eyes pryed into all the places already examined by earlier search parties, and into other places too. But darkness fell like an obliterating blanket and forced everyone back indoors.

By this point we had lost track of time and the days and hours meant nothing to us. Some mechanical instinct within us made us mark off the days on the calendar. Life had become a strange, monotonous routine: dazed visits to the police; searches around the village; bites to eat out of habit more than desire; sleep to snatch when our minds weren't desperately clutching at straws. We felt so very tired — and yet we all still possessed a life-giving hope. We wouldn't let the situation defeat us while there was still hope. Every day would be the day Genette would be found — we hoped.

Each day began for us at dawn. We had the 'regulation' morning cuppa, then drove to the post office to sort through the mail, just in case Genette — or her kidnapper — had written. Those letters we didn't recognize we handed to the police for their close examination. Early on the morning list was a visit to the police incident centre which had been set up in the village hall to check on the progress of the search. Then it was back for breakfast.

After this we would collect all the newspapers. We soon had more than the newsagents did. Once we'd clipped any relevant articles we'd plan our day's search, and as quickly as we could we'd be off out.

Wednesday arrived. It was the fifth day of Genette's disappearance, and our search switched to the road leading from the village hall to the airport. There was a possibility that Genette had been kidnapped and her captors had used this as an escape route. Maybe Genette would have thrown a clue — a hanky or something — out of the car. If she had, we would find it.

The tension was beginning to mount, almost unnoticeably. Up until now, Violet or I had stayed at home to man the phone. But that day, neither of us wanted to be left alone at home. We were too scared of the unknown.

The long day's search was exhausting and fruitless. Every hedgerow, verge, ditch and gutter was subject to scrutiny. The smallest scrap of paper or strip of polythene took on a new significance as a potential clue. Night fell, and only half the distance between the hall and the airport had been covered. We were mentally and physically exhausted, and tempers were sorely frayed. Overtired though we were, our minds still sought for the answers to all our questions. Where had Genette gone? Had we been to blame for her disappearance in some way? Had she been unhappy? Had we caused her to run away? Why hadn't we cuddled her more?

In the midst of all our distress and fear we argued with one another. It was a while before we realized what we were doing — while our child had vanished — and tears flowed as we tried to understand. What if we had been to blame?

The house seemed so very empty without Genette. We felt this even more acutely because Tania was now in the middle of her holiday. How quiet all the rooms were without their laughter and chatter; their lighthearted arguing and protests: 'Oh, do I *have* to go to bed yet? Can't I have just five minutes more?' What I would have given to let her stay up for five more minutes then.

As we sat, uncomfortably, that evening, our whole lives seemed to fall into a different perspective. How we had frittered away our precious time when we could have been sharing together. Instead, we had wasted the time, watching third-rate television programmes; arguing and bickering about petty things; worrying about life's inconsequentials. We agreed that never again would we allow the home, or family, or ourselves to take second place to anything, or anybody outside. Genette — and our family — were too important.

But the recriminations refused to disappear. There were more arguments and bickering. It got too much for me, and when someone suggested that the police ought to know about our arguments I stormed out of the house to tell them. I wandered down the road in a state of bewilderment. If we had indeed been to blame for Ginny's disappearance, why hadn't she taken anything with her? Her money, clothes, favourite toys and books had all been left behind.

I found myself outside the incident room and although they had no leads, the calm approach and sympathy shown by the duty officers soothed the turmoil in my mind. They, at least, were doing all they could. I went home, and that night I slept like a log through sheer exhaustion.

The following day, refreshed and eager to use every second in the search for Genette, Violet and I, along with the band of willing helpers, planned ahead. Another press conference came and went, and our little search party concentrated on the road to the airport, picking up from where we had left off.

We went around the area to the right of the road, and the further we went, the more alarmed we became. During the Second World War, the airfield had been used by the American forces, and everywhere we looked we saw evidence of their occupation. The place was unguarded and anyone could have walked into it. Genette — Genette and somebody else — could have walked here. There were open manhole covers, ruined buildings, underground bunkers piled with filth and filled with rubbish, water storage ponds, old loo blocks and chimney stacks. Even the most restrained imagination could have had a field day here.

It was beyond our limited resources to search

effectively and we reluctantly left the scene of such decay and waste to the police and their tracker dogs. If only someone had looked after the place better and dealt with all those eyesores, it would not have been a source of so much fear.

Returning home, Violet and I found that once again our house was being systematically searched. The intrusion seemed easier to handle this time and somehow less offensive.

I went along to church that evening and prayed. It seemed an eternity since I'd last considered God, and I really believed right then he could offer me strength. I prayed for help, not just for me, but for everyone involved in the search for Genette. It was a real relief, and I felt that I possessed a new sense of quietness and patience after I had prayed. That new peace was something that deep down I felt from then onwards — in spite of the terrible circumstances.

Just before dark I went back with the others to the airfield to check out some of the buildings on the other side of the road. As we turned to leave the site having found nothing, we were suddenly startled by the sound of something moving over an old sheet of galvanized iron. 'Ginny!' I called out, half crazy with hope. I stood waiting, straining to hear an answer. Nothing. It must have been a rabbit or something. 'Ginny!' I called again, my heart thumping madly. Nothing, for sure. Sadly we made our way home.

Friday arrived — and so did my brother, fresh from a stint with the RAF in Germany. He offered another sympathetic ear and patiently listened while we talked through our theories.

During the afternoon a new challenge faced us — when a psychic arrived armed with a whole arsenal of questions. He said he'd been out in the village and had seen some of Ginny's belongings. Now he said he wanted to talk to Violet on her own. We let him take her to another room. Time went by and we suddenly realized that Violet had been talking to him for some considerable time. We wondered what was going on, and eventually she reappeared looking distressed. She had obviously been crying but couldn't explain why.

Later we were to find ourselves inundated with psychic theories. But for today, one seemed more than enough. I had been feeling ill all day and my aching muscles cried out for complete relaxation. So I gave in and went upstairs to lie down for a few hours. I'd been lying still for a long time, very quietly, and I was neither in complete wakefulness or sleep when suddenly I pictured very clearly in my mind a blue MGB sports car with a black drophead. Then the scene changed and I was looking at a ruined castle tower with ivy climbing up the walls. Part of the wall had crumbled away and I could see the large blocks of scattered stone. The tower was incomplete on one side but stood almost to its full height on the other. Then again the scene altered to a large waterfall with a sparkling cascade of water travelling in keen, clear, crystal brightness.

Years later, I still do not know what to make of this. I have never found the place or met anyone with that kind of car.

It wasn't only the humans that were missing Genette's presence. Mouser, our aptly-named cat, was normally the kind of creature who was for ever wandering out in the countryside. He was a farm animal and loved his freedom, and would normally spend all the daylight hours prowling about his terrain. But since Genette had gone, Mouser hadn't left the house. He seemed to sense the sadness that hung over us like a black cloud, and followed one or other of us around all day.

Tammy, our spaniel-cross dog, was obviously pining too. She mooned about the place, wandering to and fro, and her sad eyes seemed even wider and sadder than usual.

It hardly seemed possible. Seven days had passed since that innocent-looking Saturday had dawned and Genette had disappeared. Seven days and a whole family — a whole village — had had its life turned upside down. Its feelings had been probed and questioned, its comings and goings measured and noted.

In such a tight-knit community as ours, it was inevitable that everyone should feel affected in some way. Even visually, life for every man, woman and child changed. Policemen became familiar figures — both uniformed and plainclothes — as they tramped around the village streets, peered into hedges, ditches and fields, and knocked on door after door, clutching clipboards and armed with questions.

No one was excluded from their probing questioning. Where were you while Genette was on her paper round? Did you see her at all? Did you stop to talk to her? Was she popular in the village? Did you see any strange cars that day? Did Genette ever talk about any friends outside the village? Did she worry about her parents? The list seemed endless. Who could fail to be touched by the investigations?

Young children, of course, suffered most from this unwelcome intrusion into their lives, as their understandably anxious parents reacted to the situation. Suddenly, their freedom was curtailed. Nervous mothers and fathers now kept children indoors, or at least in sight. Instead of allowing them to make their own way to school or to clubs, transport for every inch of the way was arranged — there *and* back. Suddenly the warnings about taking sweets from strangers became frighteningly real.

The children were particularly vulnerable because most of them (certainly the five to eleven year-olds) were not told anything of what was happening around them. Most parents clammed up as soon as their children came into the room, if the conversation concerned Genette's disappearance. And instead of taking time to explain and to listen to their children's fears, many parents bundled everything into the closet. For the children who suffered in this way it must have been a very traumatic experience — they were acutely aware that something was wrong, but few people took the time to explain. One or two of the children suffered from recurring nightmares as a result.

During the International Year of the Child in 1979, the committee identified the children of Aylesbeare as people who had been deprived of one of their rights — the right to play. As a result, they invited twenty-four of the children to the largest party in the world, held in Hyde Park, London. It was a very exciting experience for those children whose play had certainly been severely restricted.

During the early days after Genette's disappearance, the village also had the problem of facing hordes of pressmen, both local and national. They were forever knocking on doors, looking for new angles on what rapidly became an old story, asking for the odd quote on what Genette was like, who she used to play with, where her favourite haunts were, and so on. And there were questions, too, about Violet and me. Did we seem a happy couple? Had we been in the village long? Did we involve ourselves in the local community? The questions and their answers filled the papers and the airwaves.

Every road and verge, field and pathway had been

subject to painstaking searches, by both police and villagers alike. But somehow, impossibly, that lovely, laughing teenage girl, who that Saturday morning had a healthy future stretched out before her, had disappeared without trace.

# 2
# One Week Later

One week had passed and the heart-breaking search continued unabated. Police horses had been called in from Bristol and had searched nearby commons. Someone had reported seeing a silver-grey mini speeding away from Aylesbeare on the Saturday afternoon, and a huge operation was mounted to try to track it down.

Then something happened that touched our hearts. The *Express and Echo* — the paper Genette had been delivering when she vanished — came forward and offered £1,000 reward for any information leading to the safe return of Genette. They printed handbills by the thousands, with a picture of Genette on them. Some of these posters were going to be around for a long, long time.

We were overwhelmed by the reward offer, because it was something that we, as a family, just couldn't have afforded. When we were first told of it, at a morning press conference, we could hardly hold back our emotions.

The search for the silver-grey mini drew a blank. The police had succeeded in finding it, and had, as good police press phraseology would put it, 'eliminated it from our inquiries'. Their 'manhunt' for our daughter was the biggest ever mounted, and it was to involve many people outside the police force.

On the Friday evening, the police made an appeal to

the people in Devon, including all holidaymakers, to give up seven hours over the bank holiday to look for Genette. One of the areas they wanted to search was Woodbury Common, an area we had spent hours combing, talking to people, showing them Genette's photograph and appealing for help. Then the police had searched it themselves on horseback, and decided that the only effective way to search was to enlist outside help to cover the area on foot.

It was frightening to think that Genette might be lying somewhere on that wild common, with people walking past her, so close and yet not knowing that she was there. Perhaps even we had walked past her as we scoured the common. It was a sobering thought.

The police appeal went out on television, radio and in the papers, and arrangements were made for the massive search on Sunday.

When we look back now on some of those newspaper cuttings, we almost laugh. One of the headlines read: 'Police throw cordon around village in Genette hunt'. That was a whole week after she had gone missing! Even then, in the midst of our desperation, we felt that road blocks should have been set up a week earlier, on the same day that Genette had disappeared. We were very disappointed when we discovered that this had not taken place.

So one week later, the police set up checkpoints on all the minor roads leading out of Aylesbeare and teams of detectives and uniformed police questioned everyone who passed them. Villagers were only questioned briefly, as it was visitors and the casual passers-by the police were hoping might provide a vital clue.

While the police investigations continued, John Alderton, the Chief Constable of the Devon and Cornwall

Constabulary, was asked on a television programme if the police took the suggestions of mediums and psychics seriously. He replied that the police were obliged to investigate every lead that might give them an idea where Genette had gone — even if it meant investigating leads from clairvoyants. But I would now strongly question whether the police were right to adopt such an attitude.

An awful lot of psychics became involved in Genette's case, and the main reason for this was the broadcast of John Alderton's remarks. He said that he was prepared to listen to *anyone*, including psychics and mediums. I learned later that a large number of senior officers believed that this was a bad mistake. One officer actually told me that he considered it a waste of time and wanted nothing at all to do with it.

Once the broadcast had gone out, the Devon police were as good as their word — they followed up all the leads. It was a long, hard road the police found themselves on as they investigated file-fulls of weird and wonderful suggestions. We could understand the police wanting to follow up every lead — even the leads offered by the psychic and medium brigade. But was it right to devote precious police time and money to them? Did it mean that a psychic's vision was being 'investigated', while real, solid, large-as-life avenues were neglected or ignored completely?

We soon found that the psychics who came up our garden path were 'foot-in-the-door' types who, once they had wormed their way in, were very reluctant to leave again. They were strong characters who were not afraid to assert themselves. They rode rough-shod over our feelings — which were in a desperate state already. In one week, our emotions and normal grip on life had gone through a wrenching upheaval, and the influence of psychics started to have an unpleasant effect. Even when we didn't want them they were there, on our doorstep, always expecting to be met with an open door.

Just after lunch that Saturday, as we decided what we were going to do the next day, the psychic who had upset Violet a few days earlier, made his second visit to our household. When he arrived, the house was already full of friends who were offering their help. He came in and sat down in the middle of the crowded living room and began to fire questions at us. What did *we* think had happened, he wanted to know. We had to face up to the truth — either Genette was alive or she was dead. If she was alive, she had run away. If she was dead, well, goodness knows what had happened.

After some time, and after many distressing questions, he rose to leave. As he paused in the doorway he told us that all he could say was, 'It will be over by Sunday.' He said that he prayed that we would have the strength to cope with it.

'Where should we look?' we asked him. 'Where should we go?' He stepped back into the lounge, pointed and said, 'If you go in that direction for about five miles, you will come to a wood where you will find something of interest.'

In spite of our doubts, we were anxious not to let any possible lead slip through our fingers. As soon as the psychic had gone, we set off in the direction in which he had pointed. The route took us part way by road, as far as a bridleway, where no car could drive.

Violet, her brother, sister and myself all piled out and we decided to let the dog lead to see if she picked up any scent. Somewhere in our minds I suppose we thought we were following in Genette's footsteps.

The dog picked up a scent and led our eager search party through thick undergrowth and up a gentle incline. On the way we found the odd sweet wrapper, hazelnut shells and nibbled ears of corn. It seemed to us, anxious as we were for any straw to clutch at, that this was exactly the kind of trail Genette would leave if she was out in the country.

The trail led on for a mile and a half and the dog seemed convinced she was on the scent of something. She was, for we eventually came to the source — a squirrel's nest. In spite of this, we did not give up, but decided that as we had come so far we might as well continue and see where the path finally came out.

The path took us back downhill again and along the bottom of someone's garden. Over the hedge we saw several white rabbits playing on the lawn — just the kind of sight that would have captivated Genette, with her love of the country. In another field nearby we came across a shed containing hay. Someone had been there, there was no question about it. The high grass all around it had been flattened. Probably by someone looking for Genette.

We carried on until we hit the road again. Then we followed another footpath that led us to the top of a wooded hill. We reached its summit after a slow climb up the quickly-rising path. Everyone else reached the top before me — I was becoming increasingly weary.

In fact, we had climbed Beacon Hill, one of the highest spots for miles. It commanded a magnificent view, and as we surveyed the beautiful countryside, we all felt that looking for Genette was like searching for a needle in a haystack. We felt once again a sense of overwhelming inadequacy. Despondently, we made our way homewards, slipping, sliding and scrambling down the steep slope as darkness rapidly fought off the light. We had no torches and our nerves were distinctly raw. Our discouraged team arrived home, dishevelled and tired, but not defeated. We agreed that to search the area properly we would have to use a map and a compass.

On Sunday morning, we made our way to the incident room to find out how we could help in the big search in which holidaymakers and residents alike had been encouraged to assist. Eager to add our weight to the search, we were ready to do whatever was required of us. For me, however, this meant something quite different.

'You can best help us by coming over to the police station and going over some of the statements,' a young officer told me. 'There are a few things you could help us clarify.' I figured that it wouldn't take too long, so I hung about for a while as the others went off to join the search parties. Then the police took me off to the station.

It was to be a very long day for me. I spent all day incarcerated inside the hot, stuffy police station, answering a never-ending stream of questions and going over the events of the day of Genette's disappearance. I felt like an animal trapped inside a cage. The only place I wanted to be was out in the village, searching and looking for clues with all the other volunteers, but here I was stuck in a small room going over the same old facts again and again.

They brought up every minute detail of my sordid past and flung it at me accusingly. I wanted to know, angrily, why they were taking so long over these things that had no bearing on the case, when they could be out looking for Genette. They replied, just as heatedly, that it was my fault. If I had been honest and told them everything right at the very beginning, they wouldn't have to waste time like this now. I was obstructing their investigations.

We went over everything that happened on that Saturday. Every little move; where I drove, where we parked; who we spoke to; what we'd talked about; even where we'd bought our ice-creams. At lunch-time, when we went out for something to eat, they got me to drive them around and show them where I'd been. It was like being dissected.

After lunch they took me back to the station and began the laborious task of writing up the statement. It seemed like the day was never going to end and suddenly tiredness overtook me like a flood. I began to drift into sleep more than once, but each time the police officers shook me awake, shouting, 'For goodness sake, keep awake! We need you!'

I was finally allowed home, physically and emotionally drained. Dragging myself indoors, I steeled myself for the news from the searchers. Almost 7,000 people had given up their Sunday to assist the police. 'Genette's Welly Army' was how some of the papers dubbed the searchers the next day. They had marched, like 'a massive army of ants' (another newspaper), once again traversing the fields and stretches of common that had never before seen so many pairs of feet in such a short time. But like all the earlier searches, it achieved nothing. No clothes, no clues, no trails, no Genette.

But we were profoundly grateful for the kindness of all those people who freely gave up their own time to search Woodbury Common. Most of the volunteers were holidaymakers who didn't know Genette at all. Others were locals — or rather, people from Devon and even the outlying counties. Such a response from people who had never even heard of us before the newspapers broadcast our story affected us deeply. We weren't the only people to be impressed. The police confessed that they were astonished at the mass turnout. They in turn responded to the challenge by organizing the crowds that turned up into an efficient body of searchers.

My Uncle Tom was one of the people who reported for duty that day. He was a well-weathered man who had been toughened by years of hard graft, including a period of service in the Sahara with the tank regiment during the Second World War. He was no softy. Yet he told us afterwards that the sight of all those people moving across the common, poking the undergrowth, raking bushes and grass, all looking for someone he'd known since birth, moved him to tears.

Others too, spoke of unexpressed feelings of emotion as they, along with so many people, young and old, male and female, formed long lines of searchers sweeping the common. For many of them, there was a heartfelt fear that it could be *their* daughter they were searching for.

'Where next? What can we do now?' we asked ourselves that evening. Which way could we turn now? So many people had offered us their time and help, so much had been done, and yet Genette had still not been found. The psychic had been so sure, with his 'it'll all be over by Sunday' prophecy. But he was wrong. It had only just begun.

Our life took on a regular pattern, a kind of false, clockwork approach to each day. On the surface it was a step removed from any emotion and real feelings, but underneath the protective wall a hundred and one emotions were battling it out.

Self-doubt rubbed shoulders with fear; anger with feelings of utter hopelessness; uncertainty with a sense of loss. Feelings began to rise to the surface and ugly arguments broke out. Sometimes Violet and I even began to blame each other for the shattering events that had brought our world crashing to a halt.

All those things that we had possibly got wrong while we were bringing up Genette and Tania flashed before our eyes. Those times when we had scolded her when perhaps we shouldn't; those times when we hadn't scolded her when that's exactly what we should have done. We anxiously asked if we had done enough. Had we shown enough love? Had our own failings and our arguments driven such a wedge between us that Genette had wanted to run away?

It was a horrible, demoralizing experience. It was with us every minute of every day and we could not shake it off. We were constantly trying to work out what might have happened; who might have taken Genette and where they could be hiding her. We argued with each other, feeling guilty and blaming ourselves. We picked on each other's faults, magnified them and said they were to blame for everything.

Even in the midst of the arguing there seemed to be a number of facts that insisted on making their presence felt. For example, each time we wondered if Genette *had* run away, we couldn't help remembering that at the beginning of her paper round Genette crossed a main bus route. If she had decided to run off, wasn't *that* the logical point for her to make good her escape, and not half-way down a quiet country lane? It just didn't make sense.

Nor did the other theories. It had been suggested that someone had run into Genette, and in a panic had bundled her into the car. But if this was so, why was the bike completely undamaged? And if someone had deliberately stopped to attack Genette, why leave the bicycle in full view when he could have thrown it over the hedge and given himself more time to escape?

And why, if any of this happened, did Genette not scream? If she did, why didn't her friends just around the corner hear her, or any noises like a car door slamming, or raised voices? It was like trying to solve the original 'locked room' mystery — it seemed impossible.

In spite of everything, the days somehow ran themselves and kept things, to all appearances, on an even keel. The nights . . . the nights were like something out of a horror movie.

We were too scared to put out the lights, and at night we turned on every light in the house. Every light, every night. And all the outside lights were on in case Genette came home — or the police came to fetch us in a hurry. I think our fears grew from one of those early nights when we had gone to bed and were dozing fitfully. Suddenly my sleep was shattered by the slamming of a car door. I was out of bed, into my trousers and out of the front door in double-quick time.

Once outside I scanned the garden and hedges. I even went out into the road and walked up and down, searching the verges. I used to make a systematic check of the garden every night just before retiring, but it certainly appeared that nothing had changed. Then I moved to the back of the house and searched the garden, the shed, and the outside loo. This also yielded nothing.

I turned and went back down the road and into the front garden. Suddenly I spotted something under the kitchen window. It looked like a bag weighted at the bottom with a stone or heavy object. I took one look and decided that I ought to call the police before doing anything else.

Still half asleep, I forgot that the police were only a phone call away and I set off running down the road to where I had parked the car — my muscular dystrophy meant that running more than a few yards was impossible for me. Scrambling into the car I drove through the darkness to the incident centre.

It took the police only a few minutes to hear me out and drive back to the house with me. There on the front lawn at the unearthly hour of 3.30 a.m. they piled out of the cars and turned their lights and attention on the mysterious plastic bag. One officer told us, as we stood in our dressing gowns, bleary-eyed and a little bewildered, that the car that had started it all off was a police panda car. And the bag — the bag which we had suddenly, irrationally placed our hopes on — turned out to be an old bread bag, full of earth or stale breadcrumbs. It had probably been dragged there by a hedgehog or something.

The police decided to conduct a search of the rest of the house and gardens. We must have looked a strange sight: a scruffy, bedraggled group standing in the garden at the dead of night, police swarming everywhere, with a bleeping portable radio stuck in the middle of the lawn! When it was over, the whole family, all sleep banished, returned indoors, demoralized, to drink cups of tea and watch the new dawn arrive.

The whole episode unnerved us, and from then on the night held untold terrors for us. It wasn't the darkness itself that frightened us, but the things our imagination conjured up at night. Inevitably, the tales that I had heard in years gone by of children who had become victims of lust, violence and depraved minds returned to haunt the quietest moments.

Some people even told us new stories filled with horror: of drugs and sex; of dark sleazy backstreets; of cruelty and evil. It was these stories that came unbidden at night and made sleep impossible. It was only my belief in a life after death that kept me going. The awful thing was, I knew — we knew — that it was quite possible that something horrible *had* happened to Genette. And all kinds of things would run rampant through our minds at night, when we weren't actively doing things.

At times we almost fell asleep repeating, 'Where is she?' and 'Please let tomorrow be the day we find her.' It got so bad that sometimes if Violet wanted to go to the bathroom in the middle of the night, I would have to accompany her. She was scared stiff of going downstairs on her own. It wasn't just during the night that the tension would show either. If the telephone rang, the doorbell went, or if someone spoke suddenly, Violet would start nervously.

Fear was fast becoming our constant companion. It was fear that kept Violet and me standing by the bed, unwilling to get in, our clothes neatly folded and ready should they be needed at a moment's notice. It was fear that kept those dark 'what ifs' in our minds. 'What if she's lost?' . . . 'What if she's dying?' . . . 'What if she's been imprisoned and raped?' It was fear that lurked only a thought away, waiting to step in at the slightest opportunity.

Until now, I'd never really understood or known what it meant to be frightened. But in those days after Genette's disappearance I tasted its bitter reality for myself. It made me wish I could have been more sympathetic when I'd met other people who had expressed their fears.

Fear is ill-mannered and arrives without invitation. It did this many times for us. If we let our minds wander, even for a moment, we found that fear could reduce us to an irrational panic.

While we were battling to come to terms with fear there were other wars to be fought, too. As the days went on, we learnt that we had to protect each other. We made sure never to go anywhere alone and always to let people know where we were going and what our plans were. We even informed the police before embarking upon our regular shopping expeditions.

We learnt, too, how to control our reactions so that we would not make sudden movements that would cause others to panic. This was especially difficult for Violet, but as time went on she achieved a degree of control for the sake of others. And so we became scholars in a new art — the art of controlling fear.

On 28th August, just over a week after Genette's disappearance, Violet became the target for an intensive police interrogation. It seemed as though many, many days had passed since Genette's friends had discovered her abandoned bicycle: fear and uncertainty stretch hours and even minutes into unbearable eternities.

While Violet was gone, I gathered together maps and a compass with the aim of looking more closely at the area searched previously. My concentration was constantly interrupted as people called to offer help, advice, or just to say hello. The worst moment that day came when the police visited the house carrying a pair of shoes found somewhere on one of the searches. Were the shoes Genette's? I sadly shook my head. Another red herring.

During the day, the police issued new information concerning details obtained from a mother and her daughter who had been walking in Within Lane, where Genette's bike was found. They had remembered stopping to talk to Genette and her two friends. Minutes afterwards, a maroon car driven by a young, dark-haired man passed the couple, heading in the direction of the trio. An identikit picture of the man had been put together and was issued to the press, with a plea for the man concerned to come forward so that he could be eliminated from police inquiries. It bore no immediate fruit.

On Tuesday, Sheila, Genette's mother, was questioned by the police. This was also the day that the Rev. Denis Large invited our family to meet him at his Clyst St George rectory. The rectory was a large and rambling building with rooms too big to heat and too large for one country vicar to use fully. But its atmosphere afforded a cool haven from the strain of the search and the heat of the day. A bevy of reporters filed in — for the invitation was for the press too — and an air of anticipation filled the room.

The Rev. Denis Large, bespectacled and garbed in dog-collar and surplice, took a deep breath and read out to the assembled reporters and police a carefully prepared statement:

> To whoever was responsible for Genette's disappearance or to anyone else who might know what really took place on that Saturday afternoon.
>
> I do not want to know your name or where you are. I only want to end the terrible strain and distress which Genette's parents are suffering. Just tell me if Genette is still alive and give me some proof that she is. If she is dead, then tell me, and if you can, where her body may be found.
>
> Telephone me at my home, Clyst St George Rectory. I shall stay by the phone for twenty-four hours from noon Wednesday until noon on Thursday. If you telephone *I* shall answer. No one else will be listening.
>
> I promise that you will remain anonymous.

Once he had completed his statement, this kind-hearted vicar explained that this was his own idea, his own initiative and that the police were not involved.

We were overwhelmed by this one man's response. It sounded like a fantastic idea, and although we were concerned that he might be opening himself to crank calls and all kinds of dangers — especially from people who might not be able to resist the opportunity to attack the organized church — we felt that essentially it was an idea well worth trying.

The route home from Clyst St George was through pretty country lanes. Just over a week ago it would have been a scenic drive to enjoy, but now it held a nightmare of its own. Every ditch and hedge became the potential resting place for a vital clue, and every passing car was scrutinized closely in case Genette was a passenger.

The journey was lengthened by the many stops to examine a piece of clothing caught in the hedge, or a possible hiding place. Every journey was to become like this. The consequences of Genette's disappearance followed us, and other family members, everywhere.

During that fraught week, Tania had been left to continue her holiday in Cornwall. But on Wednesday, she came home. Not on a holiday coach like the one we had sent her off on, but in a police car. It was not the end of a holiday to be wished for. Meanwhile, we remained at home in case the Rev. Large should have any news for us.

It was also the day of our first exclusive press interview, and it turned out to be our first experience of the gentler side of the press. *Daily Express* reporter Mike Charleston rang and asked us for information that would help him paint a pen picture of Genette. Together, Violet and I tried to put together information that hadn't had much of an airing in print to date. We told him Genette's nickname — Ginny Boo.

We talked of her hopes, her fears; of how she had altered during the past few months as she was growing up. Even as we spoke we remembered our Genette, and the young lady she was becoming before that awful day. We couldn't really call her Ginny Boo any more — she was turning into an adult and 'Boo' was not becoming.

Tania arrived home at lunchtime. She cried, but really seemed to be coping very well, much to our relief. We had been very concerned over how she would react. It was certainly very good to have her back home. She had been desperate to come home immediately the news of Genette's disappearance broke, but the police and others thought it was best that she extended her holiday.

But now came new fears — we were frightened for her safety. Not knowing what had happened to Genette, we were scared that whoever was responsible would strike again. Our over-protection of Tania became an added problem, with arguments and tears from our young daughter who wanted to enjoy all the freedom of growing up.

As it had been feared, many of the calls received by the Rev. Large proved to be hoaxes. Many calls had come through by the late afternoon but no information, it seemed, had come to light on the mystery of Genette's disappearance. We stayed up at home until the small hours, to keep him company, I suppose. Although we were miles away from him it seemed the least we could do — we felt almost obliged to match vigil for vigil. Eventually we went to bed, leaving the vicar to carry out his lonely tryst.

At the end of the twenty-four-hour telephone 'marathon', Denis Large was a disappointed man. A large number of calls had come through during the night, but to his consternation most of them were a waste of time.

'I couldn't understand how so many people could derive pleasure from ringing my number and then hanging up,' he said later.

Some callers claimed to have information — Denis Large told them to contact the police — while others were psychics and the like. Some were just plain weirdos. But among all these calls, the information we so longed to hear was not forthcoming.

# 3
# Rewards and Red Herrings

Summer sunshine continued to batter Aylesbeare unrelentingly.

The corn turned golden and the farming community prepared for a bumper harvest. Combine harvesters came out of hiding and barns were cleared ready to welcome bales of sweet-smelling hay. But this normally happy time was to take on rather macabre overtones.

The man in charge of the hunt, Detective Chief Superintendent Rundle, asked all farmworkers to keep a watchful eye in front of their cutting blades for any clues, or indeed Genette, as they worked around the fields. Many of the fields could yield an important clue as they had not been searched except from the air. In a field full of corn it is usually easy to spot if anyone has entered the field from the roadside, because of the tell-tale trail. But the police were taking no chances.

A police diving team had by now searched 400 ponds, pools, wells and ditches in the area — a formidable task which had demanded their presence in the most unbelievable places and in the most filthy and unpleasant conditions imaginable. While police divers plumbed dark depths and searched murky waters, the reward fund for information of Genette's whereabouts grew.

A stockbroker dipped into his pocket and donated £1,000 to the fund, taking it to £5,500. His reason? He had, he said, two daughters of his own, and 'if a girl cannot be safe in a village like Aylesbeare she cannot be safe anywhere in the world'.

Life has to go on, whatever the tragedy, whatever the sorrow. And although the whole of Aylesbeare grieved with us over Genette's disappearance, they could not stop the clock indefinitely. So the annual occasions, like the flower festival, had to go on for the sake of everyone. In the midst of the flowers and colour, the craft and handiwork, and the local occupations represented in the home-made cider, corn dollies and wool, however, lay a poignant reminder. Pinned upon the door of the village church was the simple note: 'Spare a thought for Genette and her family whilst in this church.'

I took Tania to view the festival exhibits, although I didn't really feel like going. But Tania was keen to go, so rather than disappoint her I made the effort. Surprisingly, I enjoyed the outing and the chance to focus my mind on something different.

All too soon the underlying tensions were to return. Tania and I arrived back home to find the police waiting for us. My heart sank and rose at the same time. Had the police brought good news or bad? In fact they had brought a note. It was the kind of kidnap note written by children and thrown into the water at the seaside — and the police were anxious to find out if the handwriting was Genette's.

We went upstairs straight away to compare the writing with that in Genette's school books. We were sure as soon as we saw it that it wasn't our daughter's writing, but the police wanted to check it out themselves, so we took some samples of Genette's school exercise books for them to compare.

It was about this time that we had to go on a major shopping expedition, the first since Genette had gone.

There had been the odd trip for a jar of coffee here, a loaf of bread there, but until now there had been no need for a supermarket shop.

It was a strange feeling. As we pushed the trolly around, we felt as though everyone was looking at us and saying to themselves, 'It's them, the Tates.' Even now I don't know if they really did notice us at all, but at the time we felt sure they all knew who we were. That shopping trip was hurried and we couldn't get back home fast enough.

There were still places around the village that I felt had not been subjected to a thorough enough search. For example, we had noticed a wide stream running for some distance, parallel to the road. To my mind it was a place that could easily hide something pushed over the side, and it could stay hidden there for a long time. In some places it would be possible to get a car over the side and not see it.

One afternoon I decided to walk the entire length of the ditch and stream. Equipped with wellington boots, rope, torch and sticks, Sheila's boyfriend Peter and I embarked upon a search. At first the stream was about five feet wide and very shallow. The banks were very overgrown, thick with brambles and thorns which sometimes stretched high above our heads. We walked what seemed to be a long way, at times bowed down like old men to avoid the low sweeping branches. After a while, the stream gradually narrowed, turned into a ditch and finally disappeared down a drainpipe. We had discovered nothing — another search had drawn a blank.

That weekend, the village flower festival attracted more people than usual. It was the sort of attention the inhabitants of Aylesbeare did not want. Too many people were missing Genette the choirgirl, Genette the Girl Guide, Genette the school pupil, and for some people the sensation was akin to being a goldfish in a bowl — visible from all sides to anyone who cared to look.

Before Genette's disappearance, Aylesbeare was one of the places that people come upon by accident. (On the night of her disappearance one policeman had to ask another how to find Aylesbeare.) But now it appeared that everyone knew how to find this hitherto forgotten, sleepy Devonshire village.

Sunday's family service in the bedecked church saw one of the biggest congregations ever to cram itself into the old church's pews. It took considerable courage for me to accompany Tania down the aisle to the seats that had been saved for us.

As we knelt, Genette's name was mentioned in the prayers, and both Tania and I felt tears coming to our eyes. Tania particularly had a job keeping her emotions in check. Somehow we managed and as we left the church, the Right Rev. Wilfred Westall, former bishop of Crediton, shook our hands and tried to express his sympathies. Tania was still upset as we walked home, and to cheer her up — and myself too — I said, 'Let's look at the positive things. Let's not give up — let's have hope.' And so we worked at getting our faith back.

In spite of my words to Tania, that Sunday evening my spirits plummeted to the murky depths of depression. I wandered aimlessly in Genette's bedroom, still full of all her bits and pieces, and all the old questions battered my mind with a renewed relentless intensity. Where was she? Who had taken her? Was she still alive?

In Genette were all my hopes and dreams for the future. She was my only blood daughter. After she had been born, it was discovered that the particular form of muscular dystrophy I suffered was hereditary. So we had decided there was too much of a risk involved to have any more children. Genette was therefore so important to me. Even when my marriage to Sheila had broken up, it was agreed that I should have custody. Sheila couldn't bear to part us.

In her I had seen a wonderful future. I had tried to show her the things in life that were good and worthwhile; to excite her in the simple beauties that surrounded her; to help her not to be afraid to love and give. I tried, too, to tell her how I had failed so that she wouldn't make the same mistakes. Now she had gone. What was there left?

It seemed as though some unknown person had come in and taken my most precious gift and destroyed it. I began to harbour a hate and anger deep inside for this unknown person. I wanted to find him and destroy him in the way that he had destroyed me.

So the days passed, and so the searches continued. Reinforcements were called in to comb the Ottery St Mary countryside. A new description was issued, this time of a teenager who had been seen on the main Exeter-to-Sidmouth road on the day Genette had gone missing. He was soon found and eliminated from the inquiry, and he yielded no information to the questioning detectives.

I began to grow more and more irritable, snapping at people without reason and taking out my frustrations on my closest friends and the family. By now I had returned to my job, but I found it an intolerable strain. I was working to keep the vital money coming in that kept the family going, while all the time my mind was on Genette and the search for her.


Villagers in Aylesbeare decided that the time had come to take matters into their own hands. They held an open meeting at the local school with the intention of raising the reward fund and finding out if there was anything else the villagers could do to help. Overwhelmingly, people came from as far afield as Exeter, Exmouth, Tipton St John and Cullompton.

Anxious members of the audience fired questions at the police who attended the meeting. Had the maroon car been traced? No. Had all car owners who had passed through the village been questioned? Yes, those which had been traced. Had the Exeter estuary been searched? Parts of it. Had the immediate area around Aylesbeare been searched exhaustively? Four separate searches had been conducted, using thorough, modern techniques.

After discussion, thoughts turned to the reward, and it was agreed that it should be offered only on Genette's safe return. The target for the fund? £50,000. The appeal to raise this by no means small sum was launched there and then. Major firms and industries in the area were contacted by letter, and by the following Saturday £10,000 had been pledged. It was a gesture that brought lumps to our throats. There was comfort in knowing how much so many other people cared.

Sunday, September the 10th. Genette should have been back at school, starting a new term in a new form. Almost a month had passed since the alarm had first been raised. It seemed like a lifetime. Another major search had been organized. Again public support had been canvassed, and two helicopters had been called in to continue the search from the air. While the tightly-controlled operation was underway, Violet and I took time off to search an area we believed the psychic had referred to. In spite of his previous failures to pinpoint anything remotely of use, we both felt so desperate that we had to try anything and everything.

But this latest search, carried out on foot and by car, like so many others, proved fruitless.

Disappointed, we returned home to rest our weary minds and bodies. Soon after we had arrived, the other, 'official' search ended and Tania and Sheila, who had both gone to join the East Hill operation, returned. They too were tired, and had fought their way through dense undergrowth, where gorse rubbed shoulders with bracken. Their arms were covered with scratches — the price they and many others had paid for attempting the arduous task. And in spite of all those pairs of eyes, eagerly searching every inch, not a clue had come to light. A wave of relief spread over me. Thank goodness I hadn't joined Tania and Sheila — I would never have stood the strain.

By Tuesday, 12th September, the police, with the help of the marines, had eliminated the East Hill area completely. And divers who had been searching watery hiding places had completed their brief. The number of detectives working on the case of Genette Tate was reduced to 100. Borrowed policemen had to be returned.

What little information there had been had slowed to the barest trickle. Facts were thin on the ground now and the only certain thing seemed to be the very concrete evidence that Genette had disappeared.

# 4
# Meeting the Press

Gradually the days were taking on an appearance of normality — even though nothing could ever possibly be the same again. There were still new ideas and theories to be discussed, but the publicity that had first surrounded the case had died down and people were beginning to forget. It wasn't really all that surprising. After all, everyone else had their own lives to lead. But that didn't stop it hurting.

It hurt to see happy families out and about, with mum and dad and the kids in tow, knowing that my family wasn't complete. And then there were the constantly nagging thoughts: that the girl over there was Genette; that the girl in the park was Genette; that the girl speeding by in the car was Genette. She was everywhere I looked — even when I shut my eyes.

It was when a friend told me that he had overheard a conversation that revolved around the fact that 'the little girl in Aylesbeare' had been found, that I knew something had to be done. A phone call to a friendly journalist on the *Daily Express* stirred the case up again. 'Our little girl is still missing!' screamed the paper's headlines. The same day that the story hit the newsagents an anonymous insurance company arranged to print 'Find Genette' stickers. The stickers, which included a picture of Genette, were an ideal memory jogger, and the police distributed many of them throughout the country.

While the public across the country were being reminded that our agony continued, the police had released the kidnap note to the press. While they couldn't be sure it was Genette's writing, they didn't feel able to eliminate it. The press picked up on the story and within an hour of the news being broadcast the girl who had written the note had phoned Scotland Yard to say she was responsible. She explained that while on holiday in North Wales she had been doodling in the car, and the wind had snatched the paper and blown it out of the window. Days later a pedestrian had picked it up and handed it in to the police.

Some of the newspapers condemned the young girl's action in writing the note in the first place, but we felt she had had courage in coming forward to tell the police the truth. Many girls of her age would have been too afraid of the consequences — or simply would not have bothered. The police would have had to spend days following up the note as a possible lead if she had kept quiet — wasting a lot of precious police time.

One Wednesday the search took a new turn. At the regular press conference, the police announced that they were launching the hunt for Genette on a national scale as local searches had proved singularly unsuccessful. Posters detailing the disappearance and carrying a photo and description of Genette were issued to police stations across the country.

In the afternoon Violet and I were invited to go to the BBC's Plymouth studios to appear with the police in a joint effort to launch a nationwide appeal. It was a most unnerving experience. Although we were so very anxious to use every avenue that might lead to

Genette, we were not prepared for what was to follow. To be faced with so many lights and cameras, and a virtual army of staff and technicians who all seemed to know what they were doing, rushing hither and thither, made it all a very difficult experience. It needed a huge amount of concentration and we were both extremely glad when the programme was over.

Once the ordeal was over, and we were out in the fresh air, we decided to collect Tania and find a quiet local restaurant. It was the first meal we'd had out since Genette had gone missing.

We found it impossible to sit and do nothing to assist in the search. On the Saturday after the appeal had been launched from that hot, sticky TV studio, we were out at the Exeter Service Station handing out 'Find Genette' stickers to motorists as they left to continue their journeys.

People were extremely willing to do what little they could to help. At times we had a small queue of cars waiting to be handed their sticker. We felt that we were helping the nationwide effort to find Genette. If only one person saw one of these car stickers and was able to give the police some information, then the effort was all more than worth it.

Sunday came. The day of rest for some, but for us it was another day of waiting. It was a day of upset, too. An article appeared in one of the Sunday papers which upset us by inferring that Genette was dead. Although it wasn't the first paper to suggest that she was dead — and it was a suggestion we had to contemplate, abhorrent though it was — the way this particular writer had put it made it sound more like a fact than a supposition. To our minds people could all too easily read it and think Genette was definitely dead.

Although it was a possibility, there were no facts or clues to suggest that she was dead. The suggestion alone that she was might make it harder to gain the public's co-operation.

We were also suffering from other — less public — gossip. Genette's disappearance seemed to cause some people a problem, because it wasn't a case that tied up the loose ends neatly and solved the mystery. A few people started to believe just what they liked and didn't let the facts get in the way of a good fantasy. The resulting gossip — some of it started in all innocence, I suppose — was at first very, very hurtful. Its poisonous barbs had a nasty way of getting under the skin and wounding at the weakest point.

One person was convinced that I had murdered Genette. His hypothesis was that I had left Violet at the Exeter coach station waiting for Tania's coach, and had driven all the way back home. There I had killed Genette (and had presumably hidden the body) before driving back to Exeter — all before Violet had missed me.

In spite of the sheer impossibility of the kind of schedule this particular gossiper suggested I had followed, there was a whole batch of reasons why it just couldn't have happened that way. Why hadn't anyone seen me in Aylesbeare? How could I have driven so far on that hot summer's day when the roads were packed with holidaymakers? Where was Genette's body? More to the point, wouldn't Violet have missed me? It was never a theory worth giving a second glance, but even to this day that person refuses to speak to me because he believes I am a murderer.

One evening later on, after I had moved from Aylesbeare, I heard two old ladies, who were walking along the road in front of me, chattering about this and that. It was dark, and they couldn't have known I was behind them or they would never have started to talk as they did.

'Oh, isn't it terrible!' said the one in the heavy tweed coat.

'What's that?' asked her companion.

'Well, about that horrible Mr Tate who's just moved into our town. I mean, the awful man has already kidnapped *one* girl . . .'

You can imagine how I felt when I heard that — I got a sick feeling in the pit of my stomach and I wished I hadn't heard.

Other rumours were flying around, too, but the main one was that I had, for some reason, killed Genette. We also heard gossip that said although I hadn't murdered her, I knew who was responsible. Some even said I was being paid an undisclosed amount of money for keeping quiet about whoever it was who had been responsible for Genette's disappearance.

After a while I learnt to let the gossip go in one ear and out of the other. I couldn't dwell upon it and allow it to hurt me more than I was already hurt. It was the only safe escape valve at the time. But the police could not ignore it. They were obliged to investigate any gossip that reached their ears, because gossip can sometimes contain a grain of undiscovered truth.

So the police investigated the rumours that inevitably flew around. But at the same time, they were quite clear that they would come down heavily on anyone they found dealing in hurtful gossip — or blackmail. The Devon police wanted to know the name of the person who had been suggesting in very strong terms that I had nipped back to Aylesbeare and murdered Genette. But I refused to tell them. They would certainly have had something to say about the rumour-monger if they had found out who it was.

Even today there are people who still think I was, somehow, involved. I've seen the sideways glances, and I know one or two people who treat me with open suspicion. Of course it hurts when I meet such overt ill-feeling, when nothing I can say will dispel their darkest ideas. I reached the point when I simply had to let that kind of thing wash over me. And there is comfort in the knowledge that I know the truth — I *know* I did not kill Genette.

Fortunately, right from the early days, the police were very supportive and made it clear they had removed me from any list of possible suspects.

The reward fund had been steadily rising and by now it had hit the £20,000 mark. To prevent any possible withholding of information (people might be tempted to hold out for more money) it was announced that the fund would close on Saturday, 30th September. That Saturday arrived with the fund standing at £20,056. Would anyone come forward with the information that would be the key to unlocking this account?

Summer's bright days, blue skies and warm, still evenings melted into a golden autumn. As the trees and bushes shed their leaves in a shower of burnished reds and golds, they made the task of Genette's searchers easier. Previously thick woodland lost much of the foliage that sought to cover up what might have been hidden. Ditches and waysides, masked all summer with screen upon screen of leaves, now started to yield up their secrets. And yet in spite of autumn's assistance, the newly-denuded countryside seemed to offer no new clues.

On the 13th of October, a telephone engineer paid the house a visit, installing a special number for us. We were planning our own telephone vigil. We issued a press release and sent it out to various newspapers, explaining what we planned to do, and why:

> Over the last weeks my wife and I have listened to many theories from many people. All have been painstakingly followed up — to no avail — and we are left with nothing positive enough to bring about a solution to the problem of Genette's disappearance.
>
> We are both convinced she is still alive — possibly held somewhere against her will. There must be somebody who is aware of the true facts and is perhaps too frightened to come forward. It is for this reason that I am making myself accessible by telephone to anyone who genuinely wishes to contact me direct, and possibly anonymously, in order to pass on some hard facts that will lead to a solution to the mystery.
>
> All calls will, of course, be treated in strictest confidence.
>
> From midday on Saturday 14th October, to midday on Sunday 15th October, I shall personally answer the telephone.
>
> We would like to remind everyone of the reward which is a little in excess of £23,000 and is payable for information leading directly to the safe return of Genette.

The release attracted little attention, and certainly not the kind of national publicity that I had hoped would be generated. The local papers and radio stations were generous in their coverage, but of the national papers, only *The Times* published the statement — and they got the telephone number wrong.

Even so, the phone was very busy during those twenty-four hours. People called at the most odd hours, including an old lady who rang at 2.00 a.m. She had insomnia, and after a chat about the day's headlines, she hung up, happy. The callers were, for the most part, offering help: mediums, psychics, people who believed they possessed extra-sensory powers. For all their willingness to help, none of them could offer anything that remotely resembled a clue.

During the afternoon, I was pestered by frequent calls from a man who told me repeatedly that Genette was in a caravan on the Sidmouth road. He'd called the police, too, and they were checking it out, but as the minutes passed he became more and more impatient. The police were unable to obtain the keys of the caravan as the owner lived a long way away. So they were forced to break in. The caravan was bare — no Genette. I found out later that this man was only another psychic who had just got on everybody's nerves and made them panic — for nothing.

Another disturbing phone call came from a woman who said Genette had been to her front window that morning and tapped on the pane. She said she recognized Genette by her T-shirt, and gave me an extremely vivid description of her muddy and bedraggled appearance. She even gave me details of a wound that Genette, she said, had sustained. When she went to the window to open it, Genette ran away down the garden path.

This horrifying account conjured up all kinds of terrors in my mind: fears for her health and well-being, and that ever-present hope that Genette was indeed alive and within reach. It brought all kinds of conflicting emotions into play. I hardly dared hope and yet . . . The police promptly investigated this claim — but it had all been a figment of this woman's imagination. What was it that caused someone like this to spin such a tale when it could only wound again where already there was pain?

Twenty-four hours I sat — or lay on the settee — by that phone. Hope breeds a strange kind of resilience, an ability to bear heavy emotional loads. Somehow I believed that if I could only hold on one more hour, one more day, turn one more corner or receive one more phone call then my hope would be rewarded. There were times when I found that I was switched on to a kind of automatic overdrive, and my levels of human endurance rose. This is what it was like, manning the phone constantly.

The calls dwindled to a trickle and the twenty-four hour vigil was over. Then it was the turn of the post office. On the following Monday there was an influx of mail from people who presumably felt more comfortable putting pen to paper than speaking directly to someone.

Late in October, the police closed down the temporary incident centre and left the village. Aylesbeare residents had got their village hall back — but had lost a personal, constant reminder of the anxieties of our family.

It was very sad to watch them leave, but we realized they couldn't remain in the village for ever. Besides, the villagers needed their hall. But it was still a hard fact to face: the police were packing up and we were no nearer to unlocking the mystery of Genette's disappearance now than we were on the very day she vanished.

The television cameras were there to record the exodus and we were interviewed. How did we feel now? What were our hopes? What could we say? We could only reiterate our belief that Genette would still be found alive. Our hope had not died — the search would continue.

We reminded our interviewers that inquiries would

still continue at a national level. Yes, we were disappointed to have learned so little of what had happened, and we were angry because we were sure someone, somewhere, knew the answers to all our questions but was keeping quiet.

When the police left the village hall that day, they took with them boxes containing 2,300 statements, 3,000 questionnaires, and 3,200 inquiry forms. They even took Genette's bicycle, which held so many poignant memories for us. All that was left to indicate the presence of the police was a large poster of Genette.

# 5
# A Christmas Alone

One evening that winter, the BBC television programme *Tonight* devoted a whole programme to the subject of hypnosis. Called 'Where is Genette now?' the programme team had, with police permission, hypnotized the two women who had reported seeing a maroon car in Within Lane on the day Genette vanished. Mrs Mathilda Rogers and her daughter Gail, under the influence of a hypnotist, provided viewers with a more comprehensive description of the car which had so far eluded all police efforts to trace it. It was now said to be a maroon Triumph, probably a 1300, with the letters 'MB' or 'BM' and the figure 1 and suffix G included somewhere in its registration. The Rogers also gave a description of the driver of the car.

The information the pair gave was certainly detailed, even down to the colour of the man's eyes and the fact that the car radio was on. All the information was passed to the police and the details on the car were fed into the vehicle computer at the Driver and Vehicle Licensing Centre in Swansea.

Many countries across the world regularly employ hypnotism in police investigations, especially in the United States, and it appears that the resulting information has often proved very useful. But the British police, ever cautious, summed up their reservations thus: 'We have no means of knowing whether or not the information given under hypnosis is correct. However, we understand that statements given under hypnosis are reasonably reliable, but the task is by no means as easy as television viewers may believe.'

The police also made it clear they were not considering the hypnotism of any other witnesses. At the time, Violet and I felt this was a real mistake as we believed it might have brought more evidence to light, evidence that had hitherto been hidden. We were thinking particularly of the two young friends who first discovered that Genette was missing.

Nevertheless the late-night screening of the hypnotism caught the imagination of next day's newspapers, and most of the nationals carried the latest developments.

It was now three months since the news that Genette had disappeared had first hit our hearts like a stone. Although the village had returned to a state of peace, peace of mind was still a noticeably lacking commodity. Swings in the playground still stood idle. Mothers still accompanied their children everywhere and panicked when their offspring took a minute longer than expected on an errand. Every adult in the village still acted the detective, and many noted down strange vehicle registrations, eyeing 'foreigners' with unhidden suspicion. And the police still appeared every so often to check out one fact or another. Where the police caravans and marquees had stood during the summer, there remained only flattened grass, patchy and starved of light and air as a reminder that Genette's case was still unsolved.

The heat of the summer sun had long since faded to a wintry November. It was less than a month before

Christmas — a Christmas to be spent without Genette? — and we were preparing to go on a holiday to Majorca that had been booked long before all this had blown up.

We were still looking forward to the holiday — but now for different reasons. We felt it would be a real opportunity to try to escape from the pressures we felt all around us in Aylesbeare. It wasn't because we wanted to forget Genette — that was impossible — but because we felt that we might be better able to cope with whatever the future might hold if we had a holiday.

Before we left England's wintry shores, we issued another press statement:

To whoever is still holding Genette. On 29th November we are going on holiday to Majorca. This was an event which Genette was looking forward to immensely. Please return her to us so that she too can enjoy this trip. Surely you must have put both her and us through enough by now. We are prepared to meet you anywhere, under any conditions, to bring about this reunion. Please stop and think what you are doing to our family. If you need help we will make sure that you get it. Please just return our Genette.

To the public. It is ironical that one of you somewhere holds the key to this mystery and has not yet come forward with the vital information so badly needed. We ask you to think again. Have you seen either Genette, the dark-haired man or the maroon car? Has anyone you have contact with been acting unusually since the beginning of August? Do you think somebody else has already told the police the information you know? Have you noticed anything unusual going on at nearby houses over the last three months? If you think you can help, contact the police or phone Mr Tate.

I never for one moment anticipated the response to this release. The morning after, it was as if the floodgates had burst. From 9.00 a.m. onwards, reporter after reporter, photographer after photographer, cameraman after cameraman trod the well-worn pathway leading to the front door. Those that didn't arrive on our doorstep dialled our telephone number. It seemed that all sections of the media had woken up and were crawling out of the woodwork. We couldn't get a minute's peace and had to escape into Exeter for a meal. But we didn't complain. We were grateful for any publicity we could get for Genette's sake.

The following day, Violet, Tania and I sat on board a plane that was to fly us to Majorca, away from a constant stream of reminders of Genette, a beloved daughter and sister. It was to have been our family's first holiday abroad together and Violet and I had been saving for a long time to make it possible. It was strange to be without Genette.

The airline had given us a refund for that extra seat but insisted that we still retain it. Even out in Majorca there was the same approach — there would be four places laid at table, and so on. That made parts of the holiday difficult to bear. When we flew home we half expected to see the police waiting for us with some news. It all seemed very fraught.

All too quickly, the golden hues of autumn gave way to the bleak coldness of winter and Christmas approached. A Christmas without Genette.

We went out to buy a present for Genette. It was a most odd feeling choosing the right gift without her own ideas ringing in our ears. This time we had no Christmas list to guide us. Our final choice was a leather handbag, something we felt Genette, our rapidly maturing daughter, would appreciate. If she ever returned, that is.

We kept up the convention of buying each other gifts, too, but our hearts were not in it and it just wasn't the same. How we missed the squeals of delight on Christmas morning when normally the presents would be opened. We missed those sparkling pairs of eyes and the faces full of joy. All those delights we normally associated with Christmas were sadly absent.

We did, however, receive a lot of cards from family, friends and well-wishers, which we gratefully appreciated. And so none of us had the heart to celebrate. To us, Christmas day was just another day without Genette. What was there to celebrate? Violet, Tania and I let the tide of the Christmas spirit wash over us. We spent our Christmas holiday searching.

But it wasn't only the woodland, streams, fields, ditches and footpaths that were subject to scrutiny. We were always searching Ginny's bedding and belongings in the desperate hope that we might find a clue. We went through everything. We looked at every page of every book, in every cupboard, shelf and drawer. We looked at all her toys, under the mattress — we even had the carpets up, looking for a note, a letter, or an address. We must have searched her room systematically four or five times like that. And not just her room, but the whole house. As we did so, Mouser would follow us, silently dogging our footsteps everywhere we went. We looked for anything out of the ordinary. Just as the police did when they conducted their own searches.

We scrutinized her diary, trying to read something into the entries made there. We did find an old address book of hers, and on examination we found it contained a telephone number we didn't know. We showed it to the police, and they tried it out. A lady who lived in a nearby village answered, but she was as nonplussed as we were to find her number in Ginny's book. The same number also applied to a disused warehouse, and one was an old, long-since disconnected number. We concluded it was just part of a young girl's fantasy, inventing someone to go in her address book.

After Christmas, our outdoor searching was forcibly halted due to heavy snowfalls, which effectively hid any clues we could hope to find, if there were any. It was an uneasy period. When Violet and I were able to go on systematic searches, it gave us a purpose and at least allowed us to feel useful. Now, stuck in our small Devon farmhouse, the emotional temperatures were rising again. It was all too easy for tempers to fray under those conditions. In fact, it seemed as though arguments were inevitable. And there was plenty to argue about.

In the course of their investigations, the police had discovered a number of unsavoury facts about my past, facts that until then Violet had not known about. When she discovered what the man she had been living with for all these years had hidden from her, something inside her died.

And that was half the trouble. Deep down, I was scared that Genette had run off because of what I was, and what I had done. When Sheila left me, I had employed Violet as a housekeeper, because I couldn't afford to give up work to look after Genette. This was when Violet had first arrived on the scene. Ginny had played up from the start. She and Tania had both been very upset when I announced my plans to marry Violet. I had thought they would have happily accepted my news. But they didn't. Had *that* any bearing on Ginny's disappearance?

It was a frightening possibility. It was agonizing for me. I could hardly bear to think that I might have been, in any measure, responsible for making Ginny disappear.

It made me cast my mind right back to my 'beginnings'.

I'd got into the Navy after leaving school, quite dishonestly. It was something I'd set my heart on, and nothing was going to stop me realizing my dream. Normally, my muscular dystrophy would have immediately ruined any hope for a naval career. But a kindly-disposed doctor suggested that if he were to pass me as A1 fit, I could then join up as a sick bay attendant. In that way, I would avoid any square-bashing, PT and exercise drills. I jumped at the chance — only to discover that mine was the first intake where sick bay attendants weren't exempt from parade duty and drills! These were the very things I knew my body would not be able to cope with. After two weeks I collapsed and was invalided out of the Navy. I didn't get any social security payments because they said I had deliberately deceived the authorities, knowing my disability.

So I left the Navy embittered, with an enormous chip on my shoulder. But by then, I had discovered what I thought girls were for, and had built up a steady relationship with a girl called Sheila. I so desperately wanted to prove myself and it seemed that the only way I could do this was sexually.

I married Sheila when I was twenty-one — having been 'caught in the act'. But I wasn't completely faithful to her even then, even when she became pregnant. I thought I was being such a 'man' . . . And then Genette was born. It seemed like the most exciting thing that had ever happened to me. I was so proud — there was something I *could* do! That day I rushed about like a wild thing, full of my good news.

For some people, that might have been enough to strengthen marriage and family ties, but it didn't work that way with me. Once Genette was born, she brought with her a tremendous financial strain, and I managed to fall in with a 'thoroughly bad lot'. I got myself completely tangled in a web of mistresses and wife-swapping.

Around this time a further strain came when my mother died. She had been ill for a long time and it wasn't really surprising that she should die. But the sense of loss impressed itself on me with all the subtlety of a sledgehammer. We had been very close. I realize now that I became impossible to live with, as I just bound myself up with remorse and sadness, which I kept hugged to myself. I wouldn't share it with anyone.

Then one day I came home and discovered that Sheila had gone. Ginny had been left alone for over an hour, and Sheila had taken a set of blankets that we'd bought specially for Ginny. Sheila had left before, but she had always come back. Until now — this time it was for real. It was only now that Sheila had left me that I really started to come to terms with my pain. But I also found that I just couldn't cope with being by myself. And then I met Violet.

The desire to succeed was still very strong within me and I was always on the lookout for something I could do, and do well. I discovered a firm that sold massage equipment, and found that it eased my own pain and discomfort considerably. Up until then, I had been using a walking stick and taking handfuls of painkillers each day — and still I couldn't walk very far. But this particular equipment, while not curing me, made an enormous difference. Enough for me to throw away my walking stick and tablets.

What's more, I could sell the equipment. I knew it could work and was able to convince others. I began to do very well for myself. I earned promotion, and eventually moved to Aylesbeare and Barton Farm Cottage. Gradually I was able to do less and less selling and moved on to training reps for the company.

But despite the success, things were still wrong. I had power and authority, money, a nice house, car, wife, two children. I was materially well-off but I still wasn't happy and I was still trying to prove myself. I had a foreboding that something unpleasant was going to happen. A feeling of doom, of blackness. It was like having a black shadow following me. Then, when Genette vanished, it all fell apart at the seams and all that I was reaching for slipped through my hands.

Genette's disappearance signalled the arrival of complete mental and psychological upheaval for me. My blood-daughter had vanished off the face of the earth. My past was spread out before eagle eyes and keen minds, with no secrets. I had a bitter wife, a distraught step-daughter and relatives — and my whole being was consumed with a hate for the person behind Genette's mysterious disappearance.

It was — and is — an immense loss that I can't begin to quantify. There is nothing else like it. I can't put it into words, and I can't forget. Even now, all these years later on, everywhere I go I'm looking for her. All kinds of things trigger it off for me: seeing press cuttings, writing this book . . . It wasn't until a short while ago that I could look at these things without crying, and I still find I get very emotional over it.

I can't help remembering all those good times together. Those things that made Genette, Genette.

Like the way she used to try so hard, to please me, I think. I didn't always realize at the time. The smallest details still spring to mind about Genette and the way she went about the business of everyday life with great verve. They often come to me at the most unlikely moments.

I still think about the careful, loving way she planted a row of leeks in the garden. They grew well under her care, although she was a little impatient when there was no immediate signs of growth when she went to inspect them a day after planting. By the time they were ready to eat, Genette had disappeared. We didn't have the heart to pick them, and they were left to go to seed.

Then there was the time that she found a baby bird that had fallen out of its nest. Genette was terribly concerned about the helpless fledgeling and carried it home. We found a box to put it in and Genette was a proper little mother to it. She was like that, in her care for those less able than herself, and she had a good eye for those in need.

One of the things that happened not long before Genette's disappearance was her thirteenth birthday party. It was that day when it became really apparent that Genette was turning from a schoolgirl into a young lady. I can see her now wearing that long, red velvet dress, her eyes shining and her face flushed with excitement. It's funny, even looking every inch the young lady as she did, she still jumped up and down with excitement. She often did that when she was excited.

All the time Violet and I were still living in Barton Farm Cottage, we continued to search indoors and outdoors. We searched every nook and cranny over and over again and read into Genette's diary what wasn't there. We both shut out our feelings and locked up our despair inside. Every minor detail became vitally important and yet it became harder and harder to concentrate. Even today I can't watch the telly for very long without getting distracted. Nor do I sleep well. I find myself, especially at night, mulling over all the possibilities in my mind, over and over, into the small hours.

Violet showed her distress in other ways, too. She would walk the country lanes after getting off the bus on the way home from work, calling for Genette, telling herself that Ginny would be waiting for her round the next corner . . . the next corner . . . the next corner.

# 6
# Turning the Corner

Three months after Genette's disappearance, a meeting took place which was to have far-reaching implications. A national newspaper arranged for Violet and myself to meet Pat and Brian Berkshire, a couple whose eleven-year-old son Mark had also vanished.

We really had very little in common, apart from the one fact that we both had a child who had disappeared. We were worlds apart, but our shared grief brought us close together as surely as if we had been neighbours. There was great comfort in each other's company. At least there was someone who we felt really knew what it was like to suffer in this way. Here were people who could honestly say, 'We know how you feel', because they were going through exactly the same heartache as us.

The original plan had been for us to spend a short time together over a cup of tea, pose for a photo, and then go our separate ways. But the four of us, whose lives had been dealt such a blow, got on so well that we spent the whole afternoon talking and comparing notes with each other.

We soon discovered differences in the way the two cases had been handled. Although the police had worked very hard, both in Devon and in London, where the Berkshires lived, there were some aspects that were lacking. For example, in Devon we had been blessed with an excellent police public relations office.

They had organized press conferences and arranged for us to meet all the press in one go. This had been daunting enough when the nearest we had got to journalists in the past was reading the newspapers that they wrote. But it was miles better than facing an endless stream of pressmen and women knocking at the door at all hours, as the Berkshires had had to.

Another major difference was that we had received much more publicity than the Berkshires.

Since Genette's disappearance, we had, naturally, become far more aware of other cases where young children had vanished. We began to read reports in the national papers with close attention.

We became aware of the many families suffering in similar situations, and the more we read and heard, the more concerned we became about the breakdown in communication between parent and child. In many instances this was an important factor. Why did this kind of situation exist — was it an inevitable result of the television age? Or were we giving our children too much and not allowing them room to discover and explore for themselves? Was our increasingly materialistic society widening the generation gap? And if our children couldn't turn to their parents for help, who were they substituting — teachers, schoolfriends . . .?

It was that talk with the Berkshires which really sowed the seed that grew into the organization we called 'International Find a Child'. But why did we start it? A number of considerations brought home to us the need for such an organization. We came to realize the value of truly sympathetic listeners; people who themselves had gone through the traumas of a child disappearing. We also discovered the horrifying statistics relating to missing children (14,000 reported cases in the British Isles in 1977 — although most reappeared within forty-eight hours). And along with this were our fears on communication breakdowns between parents and children.

We floated the idea of the organization at a press conference. 'International Find a Child' (IFAC) could offer support to families, assist police forces, cross national boundaries, and maybe reduce the amount of red tape. We could also help people cope with the enormous pressures of facing the press, giving interviews, and guide them so that they could obtain maximum publicity for their cause.

We were full of great ideas which, in the long run, would help in cases where children did go missing. One idea was that all children should have their blood-groups noted at birth. Then, in the dreadful situation that bloodstains should need classification if a child was to disappear, it would be easy to discover if the groups matched. Such a move would have an additional benefit: rare blood groups would be discovered right from the start and recorded for future medical reference.

I wrote to all the national papers detailing the plans for IFAC, and funds began to trickle in.


Several months after Genette's disappearance, I read a book on the topic of vanishing people. I decided that writing was the perfect way to get publicity for the case, and it would also make sure that people were aware of the true facts of the case. My life wasn't really in much of a fit state to run International Find a Child in an efficient, effective way. That didn't stop me dreaming, though, and writing in every spare moment, including during my working hours. I was up in the early hours of the morning, scribbling furiously. It helped me out of my melancholy.

It was at this time that I found myself a job as a taxi-driver. Over the past months, Violet and I had become more and more distant from each other, and now we drifted completely apart. The arguments had taken their toll, and Violet couldn't forgive me for the way I had lived before Genette disappeared. The only reason we had stayed together so long was to allow Tania to stay at the same school. My new job meant that I left the house at 7.00 a.m. and returned at three the next morning. I was only using the house as a roof over my head.

Then I met Kathy. She was the base radio operator at the taxi company, and had the kind of temperament which would rise to the bait of teasing very quickly. She was quick-tempered, too. I would hear her getting wound up by the other drivers, who would deliberately goad her.

It used to upset me hearing all this on the air, so I used to call her up on the telephone and try to calm her down. Very quickly a friendship developed. I was looking for somewhere to live and I found out that Kathy was, too. So I suggested that we found somewhere together, which we did. We spent several weeks looking for a country cottage, and eventually found a real hideaway in a little Devonshire village called Bow. I must say that I hadn't expected to find myself sleeping on the settee while Kathy slept in the one and only bedroom. It wasn't the way I had planned things at all.

Kathy knew about Genette, of course, but she hadn't really got involved. However, the next event was to force her into involvement. We spotted a newspaper billboard at one of the local newsagents. 'John Tate to be sued', declared the ugly, brutish words. I was stunned. We got hold of the offending paper and read that Violet was suing me for divorce. I was amazed. We hadn't even talked about it together, although we had known for some time that it was all over between us.

There was nothing about Kathy in the newspaper report, but we were nervous in case anyone found out where we were hiding. Shortly after moving in together we found that we were continually being pestered by the press at work. The only way to escape their badgering was to keep our address completely secret.

Then one dreadful day we found a calling card on our doormat. The *Daily Express* had been to see us. Kathy got quite overwrought at this point. She didn't want to get involved, but it was now quite clear that she was, like it or not. She locked herself in the bathroom and threatened to take an overdose. She was sure it was all my fault and said she hated me. I broke in and somehow managed to calm her down. I suggested that we told our story to *one* newspaper. By now, I had realized that it was futile to try to hide any longer. I felt that coming out into the open with an exclusive story would take the pressure off us both.

Eventually Kathy agreed, reluctantly, that my plan offered the only sensible way out of the problem. After a few phone calls we managed to sell the story to the *News of the World*. In due course we were paid a fairly substantial sum for our pains. But ill-gotten money never lasts. Then, with all that cash in hand I would have told you where to stuff God, but now I'd say stuff the money. It brought us nothing but arguments, fighting and unhappiness.

As part of the deal with the *News of the World*, we had to stay 'under cover' until they had printed the story. They moved us to a hotel in the Bristol area. One particular evening, I was getting more and more uptight, drinking more and more wine. On the spur of the moment, I decided to ring my first wife, Sheila, and invite here over for a drink. She lived nearby with her boyfriend, so it wasn't too far. But when I spoke to her, she had something to tell me. She had been speaking to a woman in Cornwall — a medium — who was convinced she knew where Genette was.

The phone call took quite a while, and what with the wine and everything I hadn't realized just how long I had left Kathy on her own. Suddenly, the door flung open and in marched Kathy. She really let fly at me, complaining that I had left her all alone in a strange bar, and that I didn't care about her. She hit me and my glasses flew off the end of my nose and broke. It could have got worse, but we were both drunk, and fell into bed at that point. Later, we realized that it was as soon as we came into contact with the medium that we had begun arguing.

The next day, Sunday, we got hold of the newspaper article that we had been interviewed for. We were plastered all over the paper's front page, and what was worse, Kathy had been labelled as a 'scarlet woman'. She was livid.

Afraid that we would be recognized if we stayed any longer, we decided we would have to move out of the hotel. We found our way to a small, secluded bed and breakfast guest house in Penzance. On the way, we stopped off to allow me to shave my beard off — perhaps then people wouldn't recognize me. And anyway, surely no one would realize our identity here, this far away?

Naively, we signed in at the lodgings as Mr and Mrs Smith, and felt sure that we had retained our anonymity. But the very next morning at breakfast, in spite of the fact that my beard and glasses were missing, we heard a small boy at another table exclaim to his parents, 'There's Genette's dad!'

Suddenly we both got fed up with running. It did us

no good as we seemed to be spotted wherever we went. So we packed our bags and went back home.

It wasn't too long before the press stopped bothering us. But the various mediums and psychics kept up a more relentless pressure.

During the long search for Genette, many mediums and psychics had come forward with offers of help. They claimed that they would be able to find what had happened to my daughter. Some people came to the door with their strange ideas. Others called us on the telephone, and others wrote, some at great length. Again there were all kinds of strange ideas and suggestions. There was a pendulum dowser who claimed Genette could be found near Reading in Berkshire. Another man sent, on more than one occasion, snapshots of views throughout Devon. One even included a picture of two goats eating a hedge.

One of the strangest letters we received came from someone with a most bizarre idea. The writer suggested that a chair be taken and put on the road at the spot where Genette's bicycle had been found. I should sit on it for a few minutes each day. The theory behind this was that whoever had taken Genette would come back to the scene to have a look at me!

A dowser turned up at our house one day and took away with him personal items belonging to Genette. He then locked himself away at the police incident centre to study the items and area maps. But although he came up with a number of suggestions which were duly followed up, they all proved false hopes.

Many people requested items of Genette's clothing, toys, drawings she'd done, and so on. Some letters included prayers like the one from an Indian guru who gave us a list of instructions on where to put the special' picture he included.

Many people came to us offering threads of hope. We clutched at them desperately in the early days — anything, anything that might lead us to our precious Ginny was worthy of our consideration. The suggestions, however ludicrous they seemed, had to be followed up because they might just be right. To ignore them would mean that we were not doing everything we could.

But the promises of the psychics were all lies. They raised false hopes in us. At times, we really believed we were on to something. The suggestions and ideas preyed upon our minds, and had a nasty habit of creeping up on us. It was as though they had a hold on us which we could not control. And it was true — they did. But always, when it came to the crunch, the so-called leads and ideas led absolutely nowhere but into a pit of despair. Even a so-called 'psychic investigation team' who descended on Aylesbeare for a considerable length of time couldn't come up with one jot of credible evidence or one single clue.

I found out for myself that the seemingly well-meant mediums and psychics weren't the passport to Genette's whereabouts. And even after I had realized that their unhealthy hold must be broken, it was extraordinarily hard to shake them off. The calls, visits and letters continued to come unbidden and I had to be very firm in refusing their offers. Some were very persistent and wouldn't take no for an answer.

We discovered that the work of the psychics was not just ludicrous and laughable. It was sinister and evil. Once we got into that web of deceit — and that was what it was — we found it very hard to struggle free. None of it ever led anywhere except to despair and disappointment, misery and confusion. We had become enslaved to the suggestions of the psychics.

Kathy, by now drawn into the very involvement she

had fought for so long, wanted to follow up all their suggestions. But I was now becoming unsettled by them. As her involvement with them deepened, it was as though she was under their spell. Then Kathy had two horrible nightmares about a crystal ball that one of them had used in our house, which exploded in her face. I decided that enough was enough and that what they were doing was all wrong. Undaunted by my change of views, the mediums would still phone up.

Kathy was having terrible problems with her anger, which would erupt at the slightest provocation. She grew drawn and pale, and sat up all day and night in her nightdress. She became ill and lost a great deal of weight.

It was at this point that I knew something had to be done for Kathy. But it wasn't a doctor she needed — it was a priest. I tried calling at half a dozen local churches, but they were all closed, or the vicars weren't in or were away on holiday. From 11.00 a.m. till 4.30 p.m. that afternoon I tramped around without success. I couldn't find anyone to help.

Back home I sat down to read the local evening paper, and Kathy casually scanned the advertising section. There she spotted an advert from something called 'Crossline', offering Christian guidance. That was just what we wanted. Kathy eagerly rang the number and poured out her story to the patient woman at the other end of the phone. The woman heard Kathy out and then said she felt that the problem was 'too evil' for them to deal with. But she promised to do her best to find someone equipped to help.

It was a blow, hearing her say that. I really thought that she was going to be the immediate answer to our problems. I was thinking that there really wasn't any hope, when the phone rang and the same woman told us that she had found some help for us — and apologized for what she had said earlier! She gave us another phone number to ring. So I rang Dave (name changed) from a Christian fellowship in Exeter. He listened carefully to me, and told me that he could probably help us if we went to see him the next day. In the meantime he promised that people would be praying for us through the night.

That was really reassuring. And then I remembered a priest I once knew in Norfolk, so I rang him for his advice. He said there wasn't much he could do there and then for me except to pray with me on the telephone. He then warned me that we would need to be very careful. 'Now you've told the enemy you want to get rid of him, he'll be after you, gallivanting around, waiting to trip you up.'

I was soon to find out just how right he was.

It was getting late, and Kathy suddenly asked me to make her a cup of coffee. I thought that was very odd, because Kathy never drinks coffee late in the evening. But I thought she'd just got a fancy for the taste, so I went into the kitchen and returned with the steaming hot coffee. She took it from me and then said, 'You know why I wanted this coffee don't you? To throw at you.' What I did next I can't explain. I put my arms up above my head and told her that if she wanted to fight me, she'd have to fight with the Lord. Kathy just crumpled in a heap in front of me. The coffee, destined for my face, spilt on the floor.

The next morning, I called our new Christian contact on the telephone and told him what had happened. He asked me what time all this had happened and said, 'We were praying for you particularly at that time. We felt that something had happened.'

Shortly afterwards, Kathy and I got in the car and

headed towards Exeter for our rendezvous with Dave. The atmosphere between us was fine as we sat and chatted en route. It was as if the previous evening's worrying incident was behind us. We didn't argue at all.

But when we got to the address we had been given and I prepared to go in, Kathy changed. 'There's no way I'm coming in with you!' she stormed, and rushed off in the car at quite a speed, leaving me standing on the pavement. I was quite upset but I wasn't going to let that stop me going in to see Dave. Of course, he wanted to know where Kathy was. 'Isn't she with you?' he asked. I told him what had happened, and he and his wife Joan prayed that she would come back. 'You must be joking!' I thought. I knew Kathy.

A knock came at the door. To my amazement, Kathy had returned. 'John, we're going home,' she asserted flatly. I looked at Dave and Joan, and they nodded that it was all right for me to leave. We had driven about seven miles when she changed again, like a switch. She told me to turn round and drive like the wind back to Dave's. She urged me to step on it before she changed her mind. I wasn't arguing, and although I didn't understand what was going on with Kathy, I wasn't going to risk *not* going back to Dave's.

This time I said I'd wait in the car for her while she went in. Joan greeted her and took her indoors. While she was inside I knew she was safe. I drove into Aylesbeare to see if there was any post for us, addressed to our old home. No sooner had I got there than I had this strange feeling. 'Oh, I've got to be in Exeter,' I thought, and drove straight back to Exeter, and to Dave's house.

We sat and talked while we waited for a friend of Dave's to come over to join us. He, too, was a Christian, and Dave and Joan said that the three of them could help us. When he arrived, they talked to us about Jesus Christ, and explained how he was the only answer to the problems we found ourselves in. With great care they introduced us to this Jesus and explained to us what being a Christian really meant. They asked us if we believed Jesus could help us and if we wanted them to pray for us.

We said 'yes' — although we didn't really understand the implications of it all.

These three kind, gentle, loving people began to pray for Kathy for what seemed an age. They were convinced that she needed to be freed from the grip the mediums and psychics had over her. I began to get quite exasperated, because we didn't appear to be getting anywhere. So I did something I had never done in my life before — pray out loud. By the time we finished praying, Kathy was a changed person. I could see it in her face.

We sat and talked a long time. Eventually, we had to go home, and when we arrived we found our neighbours in the throes of a party. They invited us to join them, but before we went in we said we'd go indoors and change into some more suitable clothes.

Kathy said that she would pop upstairs for a pair of shoes. She went in, ran up to our bedroom and came back to the front door, before I had realized that she'd gone up in the dark and not bothered to turn any lights on. Up until now she had been terrified of the dark. I just stood there with my mouth open. I couldn't believe it.

That was the beginning of a new chapter for the both of us.

# 7

# A Narrow Escape

'It's now time to sort *you* out,' Dave told me firmly. We were sitting round at Dave and Joan's, and his challenge took me by surprise.

'Me! I'm okay!' I told them.

But Dave and Joan insisted. I had been involved in the webs woven by the mediums just as much as Kathy, they said. In fact, I had been subjected to more than Kathy, by virtue of the length of my involvement with Genette's disappearance. The couple who had already given so much of their time and care to us both now began to pray specifically for me.

I wasn't really too sure that I wanted — or needed — God in my life. But I couldn't deny that I had seen Kathy change since that afternoon when she had become a Christian. I happily went along to church with her and enjoyed much of it, especially the music and singing, which I thought was fabulous.

But life still had its problems. Until now, Kathy and I had been living in the same house. For me that was fine — except that Kathy wouldn't sleep with me. And Kathy found it an intolerable strain. In the end we reluctantly parted company and went to live in separate towns, although we still met regularly just as friends.

I found myself a caravan and began trying to live alone again. I was still going to the Exeter fellowship, and the more I saw, the more I knew that I wanted to know Jesus for myself. I started to pray that way. But I needed to know more. I thought that if I could get to grips with reading the Bible I might be able to learn more, and then perhaps I could make that real commitment Dave and Joan had often talked about.

Experience, though, had showed me that I couldn't concentrate on reading for very long — I almost always fell asleep. So I told my friends at the fellowship and they prayed for me. It must have worked because I was suddenly able to read for hours, even getting up at 5 a.m. and devouring chapters. After this, I started to get through the Bible quite easily.

I began to put my new-found time to good use in other ways, too. As a self-employed worker, I was supposed to keep detailed accounts, but they had got three years behind. Now I spent hours updating all the figures and bringing all my ledgers and books right up to date.

Kathy still paid the occasional visit, and one night as it was growing late she asked if she could stay the night. She did, but I found I was physically unable to touch her — not even to kiss her goodnight. I lay awake most of the night. Then I dozed off and into my mind came a vivid picture. I saw a granite rock face, all broken up with time, and there in the middle of it was a small gap with craggy sides. Through the gap I could see the most beautiful land where the sun was shining. I tried to squeeze through the gap but found that I couldn't. Then I heard a voice saying, 'That's what you can have, but not yet.' I felt that God was giving me encouragement and helping me to face the future.

I found myself a new job in Okehampton, and began the task of looking for somewhere more permanent than the caravan to live in. I soon found a small flat and moved in — although I didn't have a lot to move in with! My meals were eaten with a salad server and a knife. I had very little furniture and a bed, and I bought a cooker for five pounds.

But soon, my new-found Christian friends came to my aid and gave me everything I needed — right down to plates and cutlery. It wasn't always easy to accept. I had been finding it difficult to get along with one fellow church member, so I was surprised when, one Sunday, he came up to me and asked me about my flat. I told him all about it and how the only thing that I needed was floor covering. He said that he was throwing out some old pieces of carpet and asked if I would like them. I swallowed my pride and said yes. There turned out to be enough carpet to cover the entire flat!

I ought to have been happier. I was convinced that my life had turned a corner, and so many good things had happened to me over the past few months. But I was still very depressed. Being away from Kathy became more and more difficult and everything began to get on top of me. It still seemed to me that there was no one who understood me enough to know how I felt. Then I argued with Kathy over the phone and felt even worse.

Alone, staring at all the bills which always seemed to arrive at once, I began thinking it was all a waste of time. It would take me years to pay off all my debts. I had failed to make two marriages work, my daughter had never been found and my present relationship with Kathy wasn't going as I wanted. I remember thinking about it all very carefully — concluding that there was no point in carrying on.

It was late evening as I moved quietly around the flat, collecting all the tablets I could find. I swallowed them all and just lay down and wanted to die. 'No one cares; no one will come to find me,' I told myself cynically. Gradually I fell asleep, only to wake up again in the still of the night. Why was I still here? I was supposed to be dead!

Hardly aware of my actions, I stumbled out of bed and walked out of the flat and down the road to the nearest phone box where I called Dave. Crying as I spoke to my good friend, I told him life wasn't working out for me and I just couldn't cope.

I suppose I was saying goodbye, really. I said I was fed up and was going to finish it all. In alarm, Dave told me not to do that.

'It's too late,' I said, 'I already have. I've swallowed tablets — some before I slept and another handful on the way out of the house.'

With that, I replaced the receiver, turned, and headed for home.

The next thing I knew was that someone was breaking in. Dave cared, of course, and called the police. Through my stupor I was able to tell the ambulance man what I had taken, and I was promptly carted off to hospital. There I slept solidly for three days, while the drugs were allowed to take their course. I woke up to find a concerned policeman and a Christian from the fellowship, both wanting to talk to me.


While I was in hospital, I had time to think through all that had happened. I realized that God must have got me out of bed and into the phone box. He had obviously decided that it wasn't time for me to die. Perhaps he had brought me to rock bottom so that I could start from the beginning and work up. One thing at least was certain — that I had reached the bottom. The hate that had entered my life when Genette disappeared was still coursing through my veins. I was carrying it around with me all the time like a load of excess baggage, along with my fear of being alone.

These problems didn't just go away when I left hospital. To avoid my own company I tried all sorts of ruses. I stayed with my employer's family for a while after coming out of hospital. I'd told them that the hospital had ordered that I shouldn't be left alone for a while, so reluctantly they let me stay. It wasn't true, of course. The hospital hadn't said any such thing.

But I couldn't stay there for ever. As Violet wasn't having any truck with me those days, I persuaded Sheila to let me stay with her for a while. But it was awful. She was at me hammer and tongs the whole time. The press had got hold of the more sordid parts of my past and had spread the bad news all over the papers. Sheila threw everything at me. She let fly at me so much that even the new man in her life thought she was taking things too far.

It was obvious that I couldn't stay with Sheila any longer. Even being alone was better than being constantly under bombardment. Until then I suppose I had always, deep down, carried a torch for Sheila. But after that week . . .

I returned home, determined to try to overcome all my fears and face my loneliness. It wasn't easy, but visits from friends in the church and especially from Kathy made the bitter pill a little sweeter to swallow. It was, however, a meeting with Kathy that was to stir up all that hatred and desire for revenge — and eventually lead to its banishment from my life.

Kathy and I had been invited to Dave and Joan's house for the afternoon, and on my way to the house I passed a fruit shop. Knowing how much Kathy liked fruit, I stopped off and bought her a melon. I got to the house and, as always, it was great to see Kathy. But there was obviously something on her mind and she said she had something very important to say to me.

I couldn't believe what she then told me.

'It was rather shattering,' Kathy admitted to me later. 'I believed that God had given me a very hard message to give to John — hard, that is, for him to accept; and hard from the human perspective on things.

'He sat there, the melon still in his hands. I took a deep breath and told him that he was to let go of all the hate and anger he had hugged to himself, against whoever it was who had taken Genette. He was to let all those feelings go, and he was to be able to *love* that person, and forgive him.

'I was convinced that they were words that had to be said, although I knew how very difficult it would be for John. I was really glad to get it off my chest, and I felt a peace about it. Almost as soon as I had said it, John gave me such a look — it was as if you could see what was on his mind, written all over his face. He was going to hurl that ripe, heavy melon straight at my head!'

Kathy was right. But with split-second timing, Joan, who had heard everything, calmly stepped up and took the melon from my poised hands. 'Let's put this in the kitchen, shall we?' she said, and carried it away before it could wreak any damage.

I suppose that was another turning point for me. It was after Kathy had delivered that frankly devastating message that I began to allow God to touch the most locked-away areas of my life. It wasn't easy, letting go of that cancer-like, consuming hate which I'd allowed to grow inside. It had been a part of me for so long.

When your hands have clasped something very tight for so long it can be difficult to prise open just one finger, even if you really want to let go.

Hate very soon gets hold of *you* — you can't just hold *it*. And to replace that very negative emotion with one as powerful and positive as love — it sounded like a job for supersaint, not weak, human, fallible John Tate.

Slowly, almost imperceptibly, as I grew closer to God and became willing to let go of that hate, the hate began to disappear. I believe it is a miracle that today I can honestly say I do not hate the man who took Genette. It is not me saying it, because by myself I could never have done it. It is the power of God that has been at work within me. Not only do I not hate him, but I actually feel pity for him and believe that I can love him.

That doesn't mean that if he is caught one day, I want him to go free. But I now know that I can face him without wanting to destroy his life as he once destroyed mine.

If Kathy hadn't taken her courage into both hands and spoken the truth to me on the 'day of the melon', I might never have been forced to take stock of the emotions which then had such a grip on me. I might never have had the opportunity to prevent them from destroying me completely. Another chapter in my life had ended, as I began to discover how powerful my God was.

In the midst of the transformation taking place in my inner self, Kathy became very ill and was forced to stay in hospital. On her release she was ordered to take three months bedrest and needed someone to look after her. I quickly invited her to my home, promising that we would live as brother and sister until my divorce became final — then we would marry.

I am not recommending it! For six months we shared that house as brother and sister and it was very, very difficult.

In May 1981, I was baptized at Dave and Joan's house with the fellowship in attendance. I cast off my old life to take on my new Christian one. I had made my commitment to Jesus at last and for once in my life I was speechless. One of the people at that service prayed that the Lord would continue to unravel the ball of wool that my life had been.

# 8
# New Beginnings

On the 6th of June 1981, I married Kathy. It seemed as though a whole lifetime had gone since Genette's disappearance. A much-loved, always-remembered daughter had been lost. But with my new wife I had, in the midst of adversity, found new life, new beginnings, new love.

A lot happened to me over the next few weeks and months that constantly reminded me that someone was keeping a careful, loving watch over me. My fear of heights and bridges, which had been with me since Genette's disappearance, vanished as a result of prayer. Kathy and I found ourselves surrounded by a loving Christian community who helped us in many different ways. The Kimber family in particular were a tower of strength to us both. Their care and encouragement taught us what love really meant. Under their guidance, Kathy and I began to understand the Bible in a new light, and it gave us an insight into the character of God the Father.

In August we moved into our new home — Southcott Cottage in Okehampton. The months seemed to fly by as we tried to settle in, and before we knew it, it was Christmas. It was quiet and uneventful. I was out of work, but both Kathy and I found that the time on our hands, which might have hung heavily round our necks, became a mine of opportunity. It was a richly valuable time as it meant that we could spend lots of time reading the Bible, praying together and getting to know God better. It also drew us together as a couple, too.

During this period, one of the many topics for prayer as far as we were concerned was the need in Okehampton for a 'live' group of Christians. Kathy and I felt that the other churches in the area did not seem to have the same idea of a living, active and loving God, in the way that we had experienced him.

Eventually we saw the answer to our prayers in the form of Nick Jackson who first came to Okehampton as part of a team mission to the town. Kathy recalls this time clearly: 'The team of nine, including Nick, were always coming round for meals. I used to worry because there was rarely enough food in the house to fill nine hungry Christian mouths, but God always provided, sometimes at the last minute. Even if it did mean on one occasion that I had to kill my favourite chicken to feed them!' That time was a healing process. God allowed me time to heal my wounds; to relax and enjoy freedom without the pressures of being at work.

Early in 1982, however, I found myself a job. I had been praying for some kind of employment for a while, and I had written all sorts of letters to possible employers, as well as visiting the labour exchange regularly. Nothing had turned up, until one morning, on one of my visits to the exchange, I spotted a job on offer. I decided that I didn't want it, but the woman behind the desk said that she would arrange an interview for me straight away. I was dressed in scruffy jeans and a jumper, but amazingly, I still got the job!

Now I was out at work during the day, Kathy was left to face an empty house. It was then that the sleeping organization — International Find a Child —

began to awaken. Kathy started to update the small files containing all the names and addresses of people who were interested in helping us. The kitchen was transformed into an office.

We began to feel once again that Ginny had been forgotten, and we decided to do something about it. What we really wanted to do was to have a look at all the police files that had accumulated over the months of the investigation. Maybe we could spot something that the police, with the best of intentions, might have missed. But we were told firmly and politely that these files were confidential and not for our eyes.

We decided that if we couldn't look at the files, then the next best thing was to get another team of policemen to look at them. Surely something must have escaped the scrutiny of the police that fresh eyes and minds would pick up. The only way we thought that this might happen was to get a petition together asking the Home Office to intervene and order a fresh inquiry.

What started as an idea was soon put into action. Weekends saw the pair of us tramping up and down the Exeter shopping precinct, trying to persuade people to add their names to the petition. We had a sign which said 'Is four-and-a-half years long enough?' We asked people if they thought the case of Genette's disappearance needed handling by a new team.

It was long, hard, cold work. By the time the petition was started, summer and autumn had drifted away and Devon was in the first throes of winter. Often we would be disappointed, as shoppers refused to sign the petition. Some didn't sign as they said they didn't agree with the sentiment. Others wanted to sign but couldn't — like a few police officers who told us that if their names were discovered on such a list they would be in 'big trouble'. Still others, like the wives of policemen who had been involved in the original inquiry, said that enough overtime had already been put in on behalf of 'just one little girl'.

We collected about 1,000 signatures and wrote to the Home Office to tell them what we had done. Some weeks later, not long before Christmas, we received a reply. The reply said that the Home Office had no jurisdiction over local police forces and were therefore unable to consider our request. Such decisions lay in the hands of the Chief Constable, with accountability to the County Council in question. We were surprised at this, but it is true. Only the Metropolitan Police Force is under the control of the Home Office in that respect.

This disappointing response was not what we had hoped for. Disheartened, we decided that without the right level of support it was hopeless to press for a new inquiry. So we reluctantly shelved the idea.

Another Christmas arrived. Much water had gone under the bridge, but the deep heartache remained. I still thought frequently of that little girl who, so many Christmases ago now it seemed, would watch with unconcealed delight as members of her family opened her presents to them. Kathy, although she had never met Genette, was also affected and shared the hurt.

People tend to forget — but how can I forget someone who was my own flesh and blood? Someone who had been a living part of my life for thirteen years? It is said that time is a great healer, but it would be impossible to forget Genette. She is forever part of me.

All through our new experiences as Christians, the Kimber family had offered us unstinting love, care and encouragement. The family held a special place in our hearts, and it came as a great shock to us when we heard that Francis, the head of the family, was suffering from cancer. We went to spend that Christmas with Kathy's father in Scotland, but when we came home we discovered that Francis had got worse. The cancerous growth in his face had not disappeared as we had hoped.

In January, Francis Kimber let go of his hold on life. Ultimately, he had died from a brain tumour. But strangely, his family insisted that the funeral was to be a thanksgiving service. Although we were all very upset that Francis was dead, we knew that he had at last been released from his pain and was now 'safe in the arms of Jesus'. So we determined to attend the thanksgiving service as Francis had wished.

The day of the service dawned bright and very white. The whole of the Devon countryside, it seemed, had been buried under thick layers of snow. Snowdrifts and buried roads ought to have kept everyone indoors, but it was going to take more than a spot of good old Devon weather to prevent Francis' friends and family from attending the service. Workmen appeared from nowhere digging out the road, and local farmers cleared the route the hearse was to take. Our old, borrowed mini struggled its way through the snow, and after a long and tortuous journey we succeeded in arriving just in time for the service. Other guests were still arriving long after it was all over, so we did well to manage the journey at all.

The service was unlike anything I had ever been to before. Through our tears, we were all trying to sing heartily in the way that Francis always had. When we reached the graveside, we sang one of Francis' favourite choruses. The singing was none too good at this point, what with the cold and the emotion, when suddenly, we all became aware of a beautiful soprano voice behind us. It really sounded so good that we were all encouraged and our own singing improved 100 per cent. Later, when we looked around to see who was responsible for lifting our spirits, we could see no one. Maybe one of God's angels had joined us in our thanksgiving!

# 9
# Did This Man Kill Genette?

Another bizarre chapter in the mystery that surrounded Genette's case began in 1983. A woman called Mrs Maunder wrote to me saying she believed she had some important information concerning Genette. She had heard of us through a friend who had met us touting for signatures for our petition.

Mrs Maunder's twenty-year-old daughter, Virginia, had been raped and strangled by an assailant that year and so Kathy and I, feeling that she might have some light to shed on the baffling mystery, took a trip to Tiverton in Devon to talk with her. Her tale was long and had a strange twist.

She told us that her daughter had been murdered by a man called Ian Bealey. She explained that she had reason to believe that he was the man responsible for Genette's death. According to her information, Bealey had been driving along a foggy road at night when he saw a young girl with short hair and the same build as Genette. Offering her a lift, he discovered her nickname was Ginny — the same as Genette's. Mrs Maunder claimed that Bealey thought this girl was Genette's ghost come back to haunt him, and felt he had to 'murder her again'.

On the morning after the murder, Bealey confessed his deed to a lifetime friend, Michael Bastin. Bealey is now serving a life sentence for her murder.

Mrs Maunder then told us that at the court hearing,

John Bastin told her of a conversation his brother, Michael, had held with Bealey on the afternoon that Genette disappeared. Bealey was alleged to have said that a girl had gone missing in Aylesbeare — but at that time no one yet knew that she had disappeared. John Bastin added that he had told the police, but that they had done nothing about it yet.

Kathy and I looked at Virginia's photo and saw similarities between her and Genette. We both felt that this really was, at last, the beginning of the end. We couldn't stop thinking about it. I was so nervous that I drove home avoiding all the minor roads, and when we got home, Kathy and I stayed awake all night talking about it.

The following day we contacted John Bastin, who agreed to see us and a reporter we wanted to take with us. But the meeting did not provide the key to the mystery which had eaten into our lives for so long. John Bastin kept saying to us that there was lots to tell; that he had prayed about it; even that he had received a message from God, and so on. But he said that before he could tell us anything, a journey had to be made. We soon realized what he meant by a journey. John's brother, Michael, had emigrated to Australia.

We came home, more than a little perplexed, and phoned the police to report our conversations. Within an hour they were knocking at our door, anxiously asking us how we had obtained our information. They thought one of their own police officers had been responsible for a leak, which would have been pretty bad news for them, particularly as only the elite few knew anything about the claims. We told the police the whole story and they eventually admitted that there was an inquiry going on.

All the sudden strain and anxiety didn't do me any good and for a while my physical health deteriorated.

Kathy called the police for me to try to find out what was going on. She discovered, after some wrangling, that the police were planning to go to Australia and were treating the claims seriously. It was the end of June 1983 before the red tape and bureaucracy finally yielded to police efforts to sanction the visit to Australia.

Once the newspapers got hold of things, everything went absolutely haywire. The phone was forever ringing and it seemed as though every man and his dog wanted to interview us. Television South West fixed up for us to go to Plymouth for an interview. We had to hurriedly borrow a car to get down to the studios, but it was well worth the effort. Unlike other interviews I had done, I was allowed to lead the conversation where I wanted it to go. I said that I didn't feel the police would waste any money or time unless they felt that this was a concrete lead.

The interviewer said that there had been other leads before this, offered by psychics and mediums. I was able to say that some of those leads — no, *all* of them — were complete and utter rubbish.

We hadn't even left the studio before we were being chased by TV AM who wanted to interview us the next day. It was now mid-afternoon, and we had to be in London for early the following morning if we were to be included in the programme. At this point we realized that we could not afford the travelling costs. The only money we had was £30 in Genette's building society account. We decided that we would put this to the use of International Find a Child. Were Genette to return we would pay back the loan, with interest. It was an emotional decision to make, but we felt it was right.

We bought the tickets to get up to London, where we were met in style by a chauffeured car. We were delivered to the Clive Hotel in Primrose Hill very late that evening. We hadn't eaten since breakfast, but it was too late to order a hot meal, so sandwiches it had to be.

The interview turned out to be the most difficult one I had ever done. The questions were hard, but by the time it was concluded I felt that it had been a good session. I'd asked Kathy to pray for me while I was being interviewed. At the beginning of the interview I felt ill at ease, and it wasn't until a minute or so into the session that I suddenly snapped out of it. I later discovered that Kathy had been distracted by someone who was talking to her. So it wasn't until a couple of questions into the interview that she was able to pray for me. The difference was so noticeable that the TV crew and the interviewer later asked me what had happened to make me relax so visibly!

The police had assured us that they would give a full report of their investigations in Australia on their return. But the lack of facts did not deter some of the more 'popular' papers from publishing all kinds of tales. One reporter asked me how I felt now the police had caught the man responsible. All I could say was that I had already explained on TV AM: that in this country people are innocent until proved guilty.

I felt that the whole affair could only be conclusive if the man in question could tell us where Genette's body was buried. Then we could bury her — and the mystery, too. And I knew then, as I know now, that I would want to see justice done. I didn't want whoever was responsible to get away with it. I believe that it is right to forgive, however hard. But just punishment should be given, because in this kind of case it is the parents who really suffer and serve a life sentence.

Unfortunately, it appears that justice is often not carried out as it should be.


After several weeks, the detectives who had travelled to Australia to pursue this extraordinary lead returned to Britain. They had promised that they would come to see us with their reports just as soon as they got back. But much to our surprise they didn't visit us until some time later. Then they told us that the files were in the hands of the Director of Public Prosecutions, and that they were not pursuing it any further. They also told us that they would eventually bring the DPP's report for me to see for myself so that I would be satisfied. But they told us not to be too hopeful about the outcome.

Eventually, one of the detectives, Don Crabb, paid us a visit. He brought a file with him, but I never got to see the contents. He told us that the DPP had said there was insufficient evidence to proceed any further, so that was where it was to be left.

We weren't happy with the outcome. In fact we are still not happy. It seemed to bring things to light that cast doubts on the efficiency of the original inquiry. The man the detectives had been interviewing hadn't come forward at the time — how many other things had been missed? Bealey was definitely in Aylesbeare at the time. He was employed at the Milk Marketing Board Cattle Breeding Centre opposite the airport not far from the village, but because the office had been closed on the Saturday the police did not interview any of the employees. Yet across the road at the airport the place had literally been swarming with police. The police at one time said they were concentrating on tradesmen who visited the area at regular intervals. We had thought of postmen, bakers, meat delivery men and the like, but we didn't give a second thought to the man who visited the area possibly every day of the year to carry out artificial insemination to the fertile cows in the local milking herds. It would seem that neither had the police. There was also the confusing fact that we had heard the story from two different policemen — and both stories were different.

We were also not happy with the strange change in the attitude of the police towards the new lead. Before going to Australia, the police had seemed really excited about it. Even while the two detectives were in Australia, one of them was reported as saying, 'We would not have flown half-way round the world unless we had a good chance of wrapping up this case. We're optimistic about the outcome of our mission. Mr Bastin will not be coming back to England with us, but there's a strong possibility he'll be returning in the near future as a key witness.'

But when they returned from the trip they were, in contrast, very subdued about it all.

The Australian affair still remains in my mind as a loose end. As Genette's father, I do not feel that I was given sufficient information from the DPP's report to set my mind at rest. As so often is the case, bureaucracy leaves out the human element. To them, Genette was just another case to be looked at and judged on its merits. Complete strangers to Genette have more information about the inquiries that have taken place than has her own family. We have also discovered that very often the press are better informed than the next of kin. One reporter, Mike Charleston of the *Daily Express*, was able to tell me the outcome of the DPP's report several days before Don Crabb's visit. The police insisted that it was just the reporter's way of trying to bluff me into giving him information — but was it? Did he really know? If he did, why did he have this information before the family?

The one final oddity in this part of the inquiry came from John Bastin. The police had told us that Bealey was no longer prepared to be interviewed by them, and John confirmed that this was so. But he also told us that Bealey was asking to see his brother Michael Bastin. This raised further questions in our minds. Bealey had previously confessed a murder to Michael — was this his desire now? Or did he simply want to convince him of his innocence? I have tried on several occasions to get someone to bring about this meeting, but the cost involved has always defeated it. So the mystery goes on.

# 10
# The Wheels Begin to Turn

While I was still wrestling with the long-reaching effects of my own tragedy, I was all too aware that I was not alone in my suffering. Even while I was being interviewed about the new Australia lead, another family was going through the traumas of a vanished child. Cheerful toddler, Marie Payne, had vanished while playing outside her Dagenham home. Her distraught parents were now battling with the same kind of emotions that had gripped me and my then wife, Violet.

Kathy and I returned to our hotel after the interview on TV AM, and with the Payne case much in mind, we decided to see if we could visit them. We contacted a local newspaper, who agreed to arrange transport for us to the Paynes' home. We were already in contact with them by letter, but this was the first time we had met face to face.

The meeting of two sets of parents sharing in grief and uncertainty was the beginning of twelve months of caring for the Payne family. We were able to talk to the police assigned to the case who seemed to appreciate our involvement and concern. We helped to co-ordinate publicity for the case. Having been through the treadmill of facing countless interviews in a short space of time, we knew what an ordeal it could be. So we organized press conferences so that one interview would suffice in place of a dozen.

IFAC also produced publicity posters and stickers alerting people to Marie's disappearance. The trouble was that we didn't have any money then. We wrote a letter to all our friends and supporters, asking for financial help. We got home one day to find that one cheque alone almost completely covered the cost of the posters and stickers combined! And so we ran our first poster campaign.

Financing the printing and production of the posters and stickers was only one of the problems. They then had to be distributed. Kathy and I decided to hand them out as we travelled home one day from Dagenham. Already disappointed that no local Christians had offered to put us up during our visit to the Paynes, we were in for a lot more disappointment. We called on a large number of churches on our route, handing out the publicity and explaining what we were doing. In all our conversations, on that scorching hot summer day, we were never once offered a cup of tea or cold drink, yet we kept going into the small hours.

We made many visits to the Paynes over the next few months, offering shoulders to cry on, and ears to bend. And we talked with the Paynes about Jesus, explaining how our faith had sustained us. We took their other daughter down to Devon to give her a break.

A second poster campaign was planned for the late spring of 1984, but before they could be distributed, the sickening finality of death rendered them unusable. Four-year-old Marie was found buried in a shallow grave in Epping Forest, twenty-five yards from the spot where a pathetic bundle of her clothes had been found back in October. For the Paynes, the long wait of anguished uncertainty gave way to the grief and sorrow of the bereaved. For them, all hope of ever seeing their youngest daughter alive again faded.

The IFAC office had a terrible day — the phone never stopped ringing. We wanted to go up to Dagenham to be with John and Brenda. But we felt God didn't want us to go. At 5 p.m. that evening Independent Radio News called to ask us how we reacted to the news that the body, which had lain so close to the bundle of clothes, had been overlooked. It was a question the Paynes would not have been able to answer at the time, but we were able to put on record how concerned we were about the fact. We told IRN that we hoped such a mistake would never happen again, and that we would like to see an inquiry into how the body was overlooked on this occasion.

The next morning we felt it was now right to go up to Dagenham. If we had gone the day before, we would have missed that IRN interview. Somebody had to say what we did.

We helped arrange the funeral and of course attended. It was the first time we had ever been involved with a family whose case had resolved itself by the discovery of the child. Before we had always been able to say, 'We know how you feel, we understand'. But now, although we sympathized we couldn't say this, because we had never been through that kind of finality.

All through the day of the funeral, a song kept running through my mind: 'Living under the shadow of his wings we find security, standing in his presence we will bring our worship to the king.' It was comforting and reassuring in a time that was charged with emotion. It was a very moving occasion for us all, but we were relieved that for the Paynes the waiting at least was over.

During this time we were approached by a number of people in need of help. They included a muslim family from Cardiff, whose two-year-old son, Hosain Harb, had disappeared; a teenager who had run away while in care, and other families who were directly involved in cases of missing children.

Hosain was assumed to have fallen into the river, although his body had not been found. His mother was unhappy about the police investigation, and we tried to offer them as much support as possible. Even when the truth of the case is far from clear — or foul play is ruled out — the parents still need help to cope with everything.

We also became involved in the case of Mark Tildesley, a Wokingham schoolboy who disappeared in the summer of 1984. Seven-year-old Mark never returned from his trip to the fair. In spite of inquiries by the local police, no real clues as to Mark's whereabouts were discovered.

Another family, this time in Birmingham, also benefited from our growing experience. Mark Billington vanished one day after telling his grandfather that he was 'off out for a while'. His body was found later.

Closer to home, we became involved in the double tragedy of the Matthews family. Ten-year-old Malcolm Matthews, from Camborne in Cornwall, was murdered while spending a few days with friends in Bodmin. His natural father, Ivor Matthews, although separated from his wife who had custody of the children, suffered a heart attack when he heard the news. He never recovered, and in September 1984 both father and son were buried at a double funeral. We were involved from the outset and were able to give our support to Malcolm's grieving mother, family and friends. It was traumatic enough for us, as relative outsiders, to endure such tragedy, but what the Matthews' family and friends suffered we could only begin to experience. Yet the handshakes and goodbyes shared when we parted gave some hint that even by our very presence throughout we had helped lighten a very heavy load.

One of the most exciting letters received at this time was from the 'Dee Scofield Awareness Program' in the States which had come into being in 1976 through circumstances similar to my own. Dee was a twelve-year-old girl who had disappeared in Florida. The program was started by her grandparents who wanted to make people aware of Dee's disappearance, but its work has now broadened and it offers support to 'America's vanished children and their families'.

As I read the first newsletter from them I was amazed. It was as if I had written it myself. Their problems were similar; their need for changes in the attitude of police and government was the same as ours; apathy from the public was as rife, and their struggles to combat a growing problem on a shoestring budget were as hard as ours. They also suffered, as we do, from a lack of comprehensive statistics on missing children.

We found it chilling to discover that in the United States, the FBI enters details of 135,000 missing young people in their computer each year. But they believe that this figure is only 10 per cent of the total number of children who disappear. The police estimate that between 95 and 98 per cent of this total (more than 1.25 million children!) have run away from home. It reminded us again that the problem was not exclusive to Britain. We were glad to see that there was at least one organization which seemed to be offering the same kind of help in the United States as we were here.

We discovered that the American organization had joined forces with other similar agencies in an effort to reunite parents and children. Family Reunion Month was to be observed from Mother's Day through to Father's Day. The United States Senate had lent its weight to the reunion as had many governors and mayors across the nation. We decided that this was an excellent idea and adopted it for ourselves. We decided on a day event, rather than a month, and called it the International Day of the Missing Child.

Kathy some time ago had begun to write to all those people who had expressed interest in International Find a Child and the wheels slowly began to turn. It seemed as though IFAC was really taking off at last. But there were still problems. At first money didn't flow in regularly, and the support which was one minute enthusiastic, the next dwindled to the merest trickle.

August 1983 marked the fifth anniversary of Genette's disappearance. It somehow seemed like only yesterday that we had returned from Exeter to be greeted by the news that Ginny's bicycle had been abandoned and she was nowhere to be found. Yet five years now separated me from that last day when I saw Genette happily poring over her puzzle books on the lawn.

Now, with that memory for ever present in my mind, I had made a new life for myself. But on that fifth anniversary, as on previous anniversaries, we wanted to go back to Aylesbeare. We had never been to Within Lane, where Genette's bike had been discovered, and prayed, and we decided that now was the time. We told the press of our intention, and one newspaper came to record the event. On the way to Aylesbeare, we handed out stickers drawing attention to the Marie Payne case. Marie, at this stage, had still not been found.

When we reached Within Lane, Kathy and I held

hands and prayed quietly. When we had finished, the photographer asked if he could take some pictures of us praying — and then wanted us to kneel down in the road. We explained that we had already prayed and that you didn't have to be kneeling to pray.

In October, we found ourselves offered a new opportunity to gain publicity for IFAC, when the BBC television programme *Pebble Mill at One* asked for a lunchtime interview.

This was the first time we had been given a real chance to talk about the fact that Kathy and I had become Christians. After this interview we were inundated with letters expressing sympathy and offering encouragement to us. Nearly all of them were from Christians. Previously our mail bags had been full of letters from mediums and psychics, but this time there wasn't even a handful of letters from them! After this, the letters from the mediums stopped. I suppose the psychic brigade realized that we weren't an easy pitch any more.

Not only was it a chance for us to give International Find a Child a higher profile, but it alerted a whole new area of media interest. Several interviews were arranged as a result of the programme, and *Family* magazine, a Christian monthly, heard about IFAC through a vicar who had been watching the *Pebble Mill* interview. Strangely enough, it was an interview with Anne Townsend, then the editor of *Family* magazine, which set us on a different track.

Anne was amazing. Early on in the interview, she seemed to know what was going on deep down inside us both. Very quickly she found out all about my very chequered past. She put her finger right on it. And without pussyfooting around she told us straight out that we had to be serious in our work for International Find a Child. She said we either had to be totally for it, and make it a Christian operation entirely, or we had to jack it in. It was no good us being half in and half out.

We finished the interview and Anne sent us off and made us promise to pray and think about what she had said. It certainly did make us think.

Another surprise was waiting for us when we arrived home. Our pastor Nick Jackson was anxious to see us. Something had been preying on his mind. So we went around to see him. When we got there, his message was that either we were to completely commit ourselves to IFAC and run it on Christian lines, or we were to give it up. 'It's no good if you're not totally committed,' he told us. Kath and I looked at each other. Anne Townsend's words were still fresh in our minds and we knew what we had to do.

Since that day when we were forced to make our choice — and we chose to take the commitment on completely — there have been many confirmations that we took the right step. Little gifts of money from sometimes anonymous sources. A present of an old but well-kept dormobile van. 'Just tax it and it's yours,' we were told. Offers of accommodation as we travel around the country. Encouragement at the right moment.

The gifts of money always seem to come just at the right moment to confirm that we should travel all those miles to see a particular family. Because we rely on God to give us everything we need, we also have to trust him to tell us when to go on a visit and when not to. It might mean putting off a visit until we are positive that it is right for us to go. Often the way God gives us the green light is by providing our travelling expenses through an unexpected source.

On one occasion, for example, we desperately wanted to go to see a family whose son had disappeared. However, we didn't have any money, and so we prayed about it. We simply didn't feel any peace about going. Then twenty-four hours later, a girl from our church gave us some money, telling us she knew she was to give it to us that day! So we made that journey after all.

On another occasion, we were driving up to Wokingham on another visit, in our old van, Patience. We had been able to fill her up before we left Okehampton, but we didn't have any cash left for a refill. As we got closer to our destination, it was clear that Patience was about to run out of petrol. Kathy, who was driving, kept saying, 'John, we're not going to make it, we're not going to make it!'

For some reason I felt very peaceful about it all, and wasn't worried. I told Kathy that as we carried on down the road we were on, we would find a garage on our right where we could refuel and pay by cheque. As I had never been there before, that was remarkable enough, but even more so was the fact we had no cheque card to endorse the cheque. Kathy was a bit sceptical, and argued that even if there was a garage where I had said, they wouldn't accept a cheque without a card. I said that she wasn't to worry and that it would be all right.

Minutes later, petrol gauge on empty, we pulled into a garage. It was on the right hand side of the road. Kathy got out to tell the attendant that we wanted to fill up with petrol, and wanted to pay by cheque . . . but that we didn't have a card.

'That's okay,' the attendant told Kathy. 'You go ahead!'

Even though I knew God was going to provide, we still couldn't believe it when it happened. People, especially in garages in the evening, do *not* accept cheques from complete strangers who live miles away, without a cheque card!

No one is pretending that the going is easy all the time. We believe that Satan, the Devil, or whatever you like to call him, is very anxious to stop us doing a good job. He is the one who is behind the work of all the psychics and mediums, whether they realize it or not.

We find that he attacks us in all kinds of ways. He makes Kath and I argue just before we visit parents whose children have disappeared. We can travel hundreds of miles quite happily, but with the last few miles to go, we find ourselves bickering. The Devil is very clever in knowing our weaknesses; he trades upon them, goading us. Sometime he puts all kinds of doubts into our minds concerning the very existence of International Find a Child, and we come to the brink of giving it all up. But God never deserts us in these moments. He always finds ways to remind us that it's his work we're doing.

Afterwards, we look back and we can see just where Satan was itching to spoil things. Usually, when he has been having a go at us, we find that once we have got rid of him, our meeting with the parents, the police or the press goes very well. Sometimes we're able to talk about Jesus to the mum and dad — because there is no doubt that Kathy and I could not have survived this far without his help. Sometimes the press are particularly sympathetic and interviews go well. Or perhaps the police are happy to involve us or accept any suggestions, or answer any questions.

If one thing keeps returning to our minds, then it is the desperate need of people going through the anguish of having a child disappear. We *know* that we cannot desert them, leaving them to fight their own battles. We discovered to our own cost, what it was like to 'go it alone'. It is simply not right for anyone —

and especially for Christians — to ignore these needs and pretend that they don't exist.

Frank and Beryl Jeffries are a couple from Dagenham who were, and still are, involved in the Marie Payne case. One of the lessons they learnt from helping Marie's parents was that people around often felt unable, or were unwilling to get involved.

'People are often afraid to get involved in these family tragedies' said Frank, 'because they think they have nothing to offer. But if *your* son, daughter or sister disappeared, how would you feel? Would you want to forget you ever knew what friendship was? These parents don't want to be treated as lepers, as "unapproachables". We can give them strength just by being there. We don't need any qualifications.

'I firmly believe that everyone, and Christians especially, have a responsibility to help. It's the kind of thing Jesus would have done, and it's typical of the compassion he would have shown.'

Knowing the kind of agonies people go through when someone close to them disappears, we realize how important this kind of love and care is. But who is going to give it? It is no good offering empty words from the safety of your own home, and not acting. Prayer is vital, of course, but what if *you* are meant to be the answer to your own prayers? You could live in the same road as a family whose daughter has vanished, and pray, 'Lord send someone to help them out.' The chances are it's you that ought to go. And if you don't, who will?

# 11
# Where Have All The Children Gone?

How many children go missing each year in the United Kingdom? If I was given a pound for every time I have been asked that question, I would be a wealthy man. However, I am as far removed from owning a personal Swiss bank account as we are from knowing the answer to that knotty question. Even after several years of studying, interviewing children and parents, and reading all kinds of reports, it is a question that still remains unanswered. All I do know is that over 14,000 children each year are reported to Scotland Yard's Missing Persons Bureau.

In November 1984, we wrote to the bureau asking for the statistics for missing children. The bureau released the following figures:

|      | Metropolitan | Boys | Girls | Provincial | Boys | Girls |
|------|--------------|------|-------|------------|------|-------|
| 1983 | 2874         | 1340 | 1534  | 318        | 144  | 174   |
| 1982 | 3373         | 1550 | 1823  | 276        | 135  | 141   |
| 1981 | 2561         | 1046 | 1515  | 257        | 122  | 135   |
| 1980 | 3158         | 1309 | 1849  | 324        | 153  | 171   |
| 1979 | 2882         | 1156 | 1726  | 362        | 144  | 218   |

These figures refer to the number of children under the age of eighteen who are reported missing in any one year. As the office explained: 'The figures shown are for the numbers of descriptive forms received in this office. Many more children are reported missing throughout the year, but are traced before the descriptive form is sent to this office. Unfortunately the figures for those cases are not available.'

But even these kinds of statistics can be misleading. How are the totals arrived at? The figures include every child reported missing from within the Metropolitan (London) Police area and those that have been missing for more than forty-eight hours from outside this area. But police forces outside London are not obliged to pass on their descriptive forms to the bureau — it is left to their discretion. It would appear that while some forces send in the occasional report, others *never* report any cases of disappearing children. Only one force, ironically, the Devon and Cornwall Constabulary, regularly sends in such reports.

The woolliness of collecting the figures is compounded by the Missing Persons Bureau's apparent inability to give any other clear facts relating to their basic figures. No, it was not possible to give figures of the reasons for cancellations of cases. No, they could not give the number of bodies of children found in any one year.

What they could add was that there are currently 340 children under eighteen still missing from their index (181 males, 159 females). And in 1983, they said, 25,000 people were reported missing in the Metropolitan Police District — juveniles and adults combined. Approximately 80 per cent of these were cancelled before the bureau received a full report.

As far as the bureau's figures are concerned, I am more than a little confused. We received three sets of statistics from them in the same month and they are all different — even the figures for the early years. There is no explanation for the conflict, and it does throw suspicion on the whole validity of the statistics they have provided. Has their computer got a bug in it that causes it to churn out a new set of figures every time you ask it questions?

For example, one set of figures declares that in 1979 (in the London area only) 3,592 children under the age of eighteen were on the files as missing. Yet in another set, that figure is set at 2,882. The first set of figures says that 3,233 children were reported missing in 1981. But the second set says 2,561. I wish I could explain. I wish the Missing Person's Bureau could. Especially as these figures were received by two separate parties within a week of each other. *What* is going on?

It is amazing that there is no single clearing house for figures relating to missing children; no standard countrywide procedure that draws together statistics and stores them. This could be done in the most basic of computer systems where figures could be cross-checked and filed. But it is not.

At the closing meeting of the 'International Year of the Child UK' in 1979, the delegates passed a resolution calling for an immediate investigation into the reasons why children go missing from their homes. But now, more than five years later, apart from the work done by International Find a Child, there has been no research. At no time has any public money been made available to investigate this problem, which I am convinced is much larger than the authorities are prepared to admit. At the time of the resolution, many representatives of children's organizations, including a number of MPs, agreed that there was an immediate need. But agreeing on the need seems to have been as far as any of them managed to get.

Today the Association of Chief Police Officers is 'satisfied that the arrangements existing for recording details of vulnerable missing persons on the Police National Computer are effective, and we believe therefore that no change is necessary.' And the Home Office states, 'Of course, the existence of more comprehensive statistics would not of itself help to locate the missing children.'

It is still a mystery to me how so-called responsible bodies can make such sweeping statements when the very lack of the statistics they are talking about means they have no research to back up their comments. If they had a central bank of details available, then any such comments could be viewed in a rather different light.

In the winter of 1983 we became so frustrated by the attitudes surrounding the problem that we decided to do something about it ourselves. We took the time and trouble to circulate all the police forces in the country with a questionnaire. We invited them to help us with our research and to provide us with information. Out of forty-three letters posted, only five elicited replies and not one force was prepared to give us even five minutes to assist in our research. Just one force congratulated us on our interest in the families concerned and asked us to send them some leaflets to pass on to parents in their constabulary who were experiencing the horrors that come when a child goes missing.

Since then, we have three times received complaints from high-ranking police officers who said that they did not know that we existed. Yet every chief constable was notified in writing.

We felt — and still feel — that to appreciate the enormity of the situation countrywide we had to have some kind of realistic national figure. We also felt that it is as important to know why a child has disappeared for an hour or two as it is to know why he or she has disappeared for a month or more. Obviously, it is difficult to obtain statistics for children who return home after an hour. But surely there ought to be *some* statistics available.

Were we the only ones to think in that way? Were the figures from London sufficient to gauge the entire national situation? Or were there going to be considerable regional variations? Why were statistics concerning children in care separate? How many children go missing more than once? And what about those children whose disappearance is never reported because their parents just don't care? These are questions that no one seems to want to answer.

As part of our research, as well as writing to each police force, we wrote to the editors of all the national newspapers asking young people to contact us by letter or phone. We made sure that we explained clearly what we were doing and why, but unfortunately, not all the editors were able to help. We were extremely grateful to those papers that responded positively. The most amazing thing was that considering so many children go missing each year, only a few made contact with us. Maybe they were suspicious of our motives. Perhaps not many runaways see newspapers, or perhaps they were afraid that we would pass any information on to their parents.

We wanted to find out what it was that made a child decide to leave the comfort, safety and security of his or her home environment. We discovered very quickly that there was no easy answer to that question, as everyone we spoke to gave us a different reason. But we did find that these responses were always surprisingly simple. Young people left home because ordinary, everyday occurrences were allowed to get out of hand. In almost all of the cases we examined, a communications breakdown between children and parents was a prime factor. In most of the cases the breakdown was serious, leaving too great a gap to bridge.

After seeing so much suffering and distress in families who have gone through the experience of a child going missing, one thing comes through to me loud and clear. Parents must bend over backwards to keep talking to their children, however hard it may seem. And they must never forget to let them know how much they love them. This is especially important during the sometimes difficult and turbulent teenage period when young people are testing their parents' reactions as they plunge from one life experience to another. Today, more than ever before, with children becoming more 'adult' at a younger and younger age, and under constant pressure from advertising, television, films and video, it is vital that children are able to communicate with someone. Television can never take the place of a person.

Once a child of under sixteen makes that first break and leaves home, they become easy prey for people involved in crime and the more unsavoury side of life. One young man from Belgium who ran away at the age of eleven and never returned home, now works with runaways and drug addicts in Amsterdam. He told me, 'In the first few days, the runaway needs help for food, shelter and drink. Their future from that moment depends entirely on who they approach and ask for help.' This became more obvious as we interviewed more and more people.

How did we find so many people to interview? When Genette vanished, her disappearance received an enormous amount of interest right from the word go. Naturally I saved all the press cuttings. Gradually, I started to collect cuttings concerning other children who had disappeared, and where possible we contacted the affected families to offer the assistance of

IFAC. Slowly our case histories file began to grow, and often, if the children returned home, they were glad to talk to us in the hope that other young people might be put off falling into the same difficulties. In all the conversations I have had with these children, I can only remember one person saying she would leave home again.

Once we had made contact with those children and parents who were willing to talk, we sent them a questionnaire designed to highlight any dominant factors for the child leaving. We hoped that the answers to the questionnaire would indicate major factors in disappearances. This would give us something to work on with a view to eliminating those factors. However, although we did find some things that deserved highlighting, the whole problem began to emerge as something far more complex than we had ever imagined.

Common factors did not come to the surface in the way that we had hoped — except, perhaps, the communications breakdown between parents and children. Every case was different and unique in its own special way, and we realized that it was going to be impossible to generalize.

To give some idea of the diversity of experiences we decided to include some of the case histories that we came across. The names of those involved have been changed to protect their privacy, and locations have been altered.

All the stories — however incredible they may seem — are accurate and authentic.

# 12
# Runaways and Hideaways

**Sue**
Sue was an attractive teenager whose long blonde hair reached her shoulders. Her appealing blue eyes and slim, well proportioned figure, coupled with her lively, well-educated chatter, earmarked her as someone who should never need to be without friends.

One spring night, at 11.30 p.m., Sue closed the front door behind her, taking with her just enough money for her bus fare into the West End, and the entrance fee for the disco she and her friend Anne were heading for. The two girls met up at the bus stop as planned and, chatting about the night ahead, found a seat at the front of the bus's top deck.

The bus crawled through the night traffic of taxis and buses. The girls clattered down the stairs in their sling-back shoes as the bus pulled up at their destination.

Sue and Anne headed down the road and round the corner towards the Cellar Disco where the lights flashed invitingly. From under the pavement came the steady 'thump, thump' of the disco music.

A flight of a dozen or so steps took them into the smoke-filled basement and into the heart of the disco. The two girls soon became accustomed to the low, flashing lights and constant noise, and began to dance. They were both attractive and there was no shortage of young men eager to dance with them and vie for the chance to buy them drinks.

As the night turned to morning the disco gradually emptied, leaving only a few people scattered about the room. Sue and Anne also remained. A man in his late thirties, but looking younger, had befriended the vulnerable teenagers, and Sue particularly was not averse to his attentions.

Dave, as he had introduced himself, was tall and slim with brown eyes and well-cut light brown hair. He seemed to the girls to be a nice, well-mannered man who really cared about them. Dave, however, was used to appearing in this way to such young, inexperienced girls, who could well prove to be the passport to a good few meal tickets. He had marked the girls out as 'possible new business' early in the evening, and he had invested in it with soft talk, a few dances and a steady flow of drink.

Now the time had come to see if all his hard work was going to pay off. He was pretty sure he was backing a pair of winners this time.

Flattered by the attentions of this beguiling man, Sue and Anne forgot all thoughts of home. When Dave casually asked if they had anywhere to stay the night, they both shook their heads. It was all so easy for Dave. He invited them both to come back to his flat for the night. Sue and Anne realized that the invitation would probably include more than a nightcap, but they both accepted.

When Sue woke up, the next morning, she was in bed with the smooth-talking, persuasive Dave. The grey, misty dawn of another April day stretched across the horizon, and it brought the dawn of a new way of life for Sue. It was to be a life that would lead her into dangerous and bizarre experiences.

As Sue lay in the warmth of the bed, her mind went back to her home and to the old routine she knew so well: getting up and preparing for school . . . the walk to the corner where the school bus made its regular morning pickup . . . the constant nagging by all the teachers to 'revise, revise, revise' . . . Surely there was more to life than revising? It seemed as if the teachers had given up teaching. Sue had read her notes over and over again but wanted something new to occupy her mind. This was more like it — she knew she was too old to go to school anymore.

Dave stirred beside her and Sue looked down at this man who she thought was so wonderful. This, she thought, was it. She was in love. She was also underage.

That week unlocked 101 new doors for Sue — it was like living in a different world. Dave took enormous trouble to be kind to her — helping her select the right accessories to match the dresses he bought her and gradually transforming her from a gauche, teenage schoolgirl into a sophisticated young woman. Sue didn't believe that she could be so happy. But this was all to change, very soon.

At the end of the week a subtle transformation began to overtake Dave. He began to appear to be concerned about money. How was he going to pay for this, or for that? And what was he going to do with all the bills that were coming in? It didn't take Dave long to make himself abundantly clear. Sue had got to start paying her own way — by becoming a prostitute. At first, Sue was horrified and could not quite believe what Dave was expecting her to do. It took a string of threats from 'wonderful' Dave and several heated arguments to get her to see his way of thinking.

At first, Dave followed Sue and another of his recruits everywhere. Sue was too scared to do anything but what she was told. This was a new world all right — and she was beginning to wish she'd never met Dave. On her first day on the streets, Sue went to bed with two 'clients', taking her earnings back to Dave.

The next day, Dave sent her out alone to walk the streets of a particularly notorious area of London. Nervously she paced the pavement. She hadn't been there for long when she met a cinema club employee. Pete offered to help her and seemed to Sue an ideal escape route. Pete drove her back to Dave's flat, where they collected a few of Sue's belongings. As they left the flat behind them, Pete promised to introduce her to an escort agency.

As Sue commented later, 'Once I had started it was all so easy.' Once introduced to the agency Sue continued walking the streets and slipped into a new kind of routine. Selling sex became less of a nightmare, and although she was occasionally troubled by pangs of conscience, it was all too easy to continue.

'I sometimes wondered how I'd ever allowed myself to get into this horrible trap,' said Sue. 'But those thoughts seemed to disappear as quickly as they came.'

Now she was an 'official' escort girl, Sue was expected to check in for work at six each evening. By midnight she could expect to have earned over £100 in cash, just by putting on an act and 'being nice' for a few hours. All that was required of her was that she was polite to the client, let him wine and dine her and accompany him back to a hotel.

Most of her clients were Arabs, who were extremely wealthy. Often their suites were in exclusive hotels like the Hilton, Grosvenor House and Park Lane. Sue would give the agency £20 each night and the rest went into Pete's pocket. He would give Sue a small amount to spend.

One night, Sue was walking her usual patch when she turned a corner — and walked straight into Dave. He reacted quickly. Grabbing hold of her arm, he dragged her into an alleyway off the main street. There, covered by darkness, he systematically and brutally beat her until she was black and blue all over. Then, as she lay shaking and sobbing soundlessly, Dave aimed one last kick at the heap in the gutter, and melted away into the darkness. It was a while before Sue was back on the streets again, and it was even longer before the cuts healed and the bruises disappeared.

Even without the danger of encountering Dave again, Sue was still to find herself in other situations, just as dangerous. Sometimes, for example, she found herself a virtual prisoner in hotel rooms.

'You couldn't call for help, because if you did you would get into trouble with the hotel people for being there in the first place. Some of the Arab clients could be quite ruthless in their efforts to keep you there.'

One night, as one such Arab refused to let Sue leave, she threatened to rip the telephone off the wall in an effort to frighten him. He called her bluff and Sue, who was now beginning to feel scared, carried out her threat. Still the angry man refused to unlock the door. It took a lot of talking and persuading before he relented and allowed her to leave.

Worse was to follow. After several close shaves with some of the clients, Sue began to carry a knife with her, for protection. One night, the now-familiar pattern emerged, as the Arab gentleman Sue had spent the evening with began to show signs of violence, refusing to let her leave. It was about 4.00 a.m. and as far as Sue was concerned enough was enough. And in this case she had suffered more than enough. In spite of her gentle talking and explanations that she had to leave, he grew rougher and more abusive. In desperation Sue pulled out her knife and plunged it into his arm. At once his grip on Sue relaxed and he fell to the floor clutching his arm. As he lay groaning with the pain, the terrified Sue snatched the key, unlocked the door and ran.

A great deal seemed to have packed itself into those few weeks since that visit to the disco. After about four months of this knife-edge existence, Sue decided to phone her mother. At first her mum shouted at her — she had been so terribly worried, not knowing whether Sue was alive or dead. This came as a shock to Sue, who hadn't realized what her parents were going through. She hadn't given their fears a second thought.

After that initial phone call, Sue found herself ringing home occasionally, to reassure her mum that she was quite safe. Her mother was pretty sure she knew the seamy world her precious daughter had become involved in, and tried to persuade her to come home. Sue, however, was very involved with Pete, and the idea of being separated from him did not appeal to her. Her mother would certainly not allow Pete to live with her under the same roof. She had also grown to like the bright lights and expensive hotel suites, although deep down she hated the work she was doing.

One day it all became too much for Sue and she realized she couldn't stay away from home anymore. Buying a special heart-shaped cake as a present for her mother, she hailed a taxi and arrived on the doorstep. The taxi ride cost £10 — a far cry from the bus fare she had used to make that ride to the disco.

Sue's mother was overjoyed to see her again. The reunited couple talked and talked for hours. Sue began to realize for the first time that here was someone who had not only fed and clothed her for years, but who also cared very deeply and was trying hard to understand why Sue had done what she had done. It was this realization that decided Sue. She would stay at home now she was here and try to settle down to a more secure way of life. To Sue's surprise, her mother was keen to allow her relationship with Pete to continue.

Life looked all set to settle into a new kind of routine. But two weeks after her return home, Sue discovered she was pregnant. Her first reaction was one of joy — she was going to be a mother, and Pete a father! But Sue's mum didn't see it that way. She broke down and cried when she heard the news. She didn't feel able to cope any longer. The stress of not knowing where her daughter had disappeared to had taken its toll and this latest news was the last straw. She told Sue that if she wanted to stay at home she would have to have an abortion.

Eventually Sue bowed to the pressure and an abortion was arranged. Despite all that she had been through, Sue felt it was the worst decision she had ever made. She still regrets it.

Sue has now settled into a regular job. She lives with her mother, who has become her best friend. She's not without problems, especially when it comes to boyfriends — but she is slowly learning to overcome her problems. The past has left its almost irradicable mark. Sue also spends many hours of her spare time talking to young people like herself, in an effort to prevent them from falling into the same trap.

Sue's story highlights a widespread problem. We have met a number of girls who ran away from home and ended up as prostitutes. A walk around certain areas of London, for example, will reinforce this idea for anyone who is not convinced that we are right. There are many under-aged children (they may have adult bodies but they are still children) who are walking the streets every night and who have missed completing their childhood. They have taken a short cut into the adult world. And somewhere, behind them all, is a home. Do the parents know where their children have gone? Are they on some police force's missing persons book, in a file that hasn't been closed? Will their parents ever know the truth?

## Joanna

The country was in the tight grip of winter. Joanna, a fourteen-year-old schoolgirl who lived in West Cornwall, was in the throes of teenage rebellion. She was often absent from school. She stayed out late, escaping through the bathroom window at night. And she had got into the habit of stealing money from her father.

Everything came to a head, as far as Joanna was concerned, one winter evening. A terrible school report arrived, Joanna's mother found the hidden cigarette packets in the bedroom, and her father decided that it had to be Joanna who was pocketing the money that kept disappearing from his wallet and jacket. When Joanna came home, she knew that something was wrong. But instead of tackling the problem there and then, Joanna's parents sent her to bed with a stern promise that everything would be dealt with in the morning. That move was one that was to cost Joanna's parents almost a year and a half of anguish.

'I got up really early that morning,' said Joanna. 'My father had already gone to work. I quietly collected a few belongings together in a carrier bag and made my way down the garden path. As I got to the gate, I turned around and looked back at the house. I was hoping desperately that someone would see me and shout at me to come back. No one did.'

Joanna made her way to the station where she bought a train ticket to Truro. It was the furthest she could get with the small amount of money she had. From Truro station she walked some distance to the nearest major road and thumbed a lift. She had only been waiting a while when a lorry driver stopped and said he would take her to Northampton.

Once in Northampton, the driver pulled into a transport cafe. There, Joanna was drawn into conversation with another girl, and feeling she could trust her, told her everything. Joanna and Sarah agreed that they should stay together. They hitched a lift with another lorry driver to Dover. When they arrived at the port, it was late. Joanna was worried about what they were going to do next. But Sarah was relaxed and told Joanna that they were going to spend the night in a hotel. She had plenty of money, she said, and she would pay. To Joanna's amazement, Sarah proceeded to show her a small case she was carrying. It was stuffed with money — more than £1,000. Joanna never discovered where all that money had come from.

The following day the lorry driver who had driven them to Dover said he was going to Italy to make a delivery — did the girls want to accompany him? It seemed like too good an opportunity to miss and they didn't hesitate to say yes. Sarah seemed prepared for this kind of thing. There was a problem, though. Joanna had no passport or official papers.

After a few minutes' thought, the lorry driver told Joanna he would smuggle her through all the customs and border checkpoints by hiding her in a sleeping bag and blankets. So the three of them drove onto the ferry.

'It was a fantastic journey,' recalled Joanna. 'Especially the route through the Alps with all that snow. It was pretty scary, too, at times, when we went through all the border checkpoints.'

After the lorry had delivered its goods, the driver

took the girls into Venice where he introduced Joanna to his friends as his daughter. After a short stop there, it was time to return to England. This time the girls persuaded the driver to deliver them to London. There, the two split up. Joanna went to west Wales, and then hitched her way over to southern Ireland. There, she found herself a job as a barmaid, living in. At last Joanna found something she could do well. Her employers, pleased with the way she took to the work, realized that she was a valuable asset. They soon promoted her to the position of restaurant waitress.

Fourteen months had passed since Joanna had slipped away from home in the early morning light. She'd given very little thought to the home she had left behind. Now, settled and employed, Joanna began to think about her parents, her schoolfriends and relations. What were they doing now? She began to feel homesick. Almost on impulse she dialled her parents' home number and talked to her mother long enough to convince her that she was alive and well. But she refused to tell her mother where she was.

That telephone call was to be the first of many, as Joanna came to rely on a regular link with home. Eventually even that contact was less than enough for Joanna. She was going to go home.

Her parents could hardly believe it, but they promised to pick her up from the ferry port. They arrived on time and anxiously began surveying the hurrying passengers for sight of their daughter. Time came and went, and still there was no sign of their long-lost daughter. Had they waited this long only to have their hopes raised for nothing?

They had almost given up when a policeman approached them. They feared the worst. But the policeman explained that the car driver who had given Joanna a lift to the ferry had attempted to rape her, and had beaten her up. She was all right, but would be on a later ferry.

When Joanna finally arrived home, there were tears and hugs all around. But things were not to end there. Joanna had enjoyed many months of independence, fending for herself. Trying to readapt to the family routine was a much greater strain than parents and daughter could ever have anticipated. Joanna soon realized that if she was to maintain a healthy relationship with her parents, she would have to leave home. She now lives just round the corner from her parents with her husband and daughter.

This particular case raises many questions. How did Joanna manage to remain undetected as she travelled from country to country when the police are so insistent that it is impossible for children to leave the United Kingdom unless they have all the correct papers? What possessed the lorry driver to be involved to such an extent when he must have been sure that the girls were under-age, and almost certainly runaways? Where did Sarah, Joanna's friend, get all that money from? Had she been involved in some kind of crime? And what became of Sarah — is she even now causing a family somewhere great heartache because she is nowhere to be found? We will probably never know.

### Andrew

Andrew was a happy boy who was brought up in a secure, respectable home. He was quiet, shy and hardworking, and loved the small, quiet school which had an excellent reputation in the area. There seemed nothing in his life that would be likely to force him to run away from home. He was likely neither to get into serious trouble at school nor to fall in with the wrong kind of company.

It was when Andrew's father gained promotion, and the family had to move as a result, that things started to go wrong. Not only did Andrew have to get used to a new home, he also had to cope with a new school. This one was a far cry from the school where he had fitted in so well. It was a large comprehensive school with a rough and ready reputation, and a different kind of approach to discipline.

Andrew was approaching puberty and was acutely shy of the changes he was experiencing. But at his new school he was expected to wear only shorts and plimsolls for his PE lessons. He was so used to wearing full kit — including a shirt or vest — that the new way of doing things came as a shock to him.

One day during gym, he refused to remove his vest. The brusque master threatened him with the cane if he continued to disobey. Andrew was despatched to the changing rooms with a command to remove his vest, but instead of meekly following his instructions, he ran into the lavatory where he changed back into his school uniform. Once dressed, he slipped out of one of the side doors of the school and ran off down the road.

At first he took little notice of where he was going — all he wanted to do was get away from the new school and all the frightening things it represented. Gradually he began to think a little more coherently, and decided to head for the area where he used to live. That's where his security seemed to lie.

It was quite a walk, but the weather was fine and the sunshine and blue sky began to restore Andrew's crushed spirit. Eventually he arrived in the street where he used to live. Standing and surveying the familiar scene, Andrew was suddenly struck by the realization that he had walked all this way. It was getting late and he had nowhere to stay — no food and no bed for the night.

The best thing to do, he decided, was to go to find someone he knew. The most obvious person he could think of was the youth leader of the club he used to attend on Friday nights before he had moved. Fortunately for Andrew, Mike was at home, and he was quick to find out what had happened. They talked about the problem for some time and somehow it didn't seem quite so bad to Andrew any more. Then Mike called Andrew's parents and offered to run him home. Before another hour had passed, Andrew was reunited with his parents and was promised that there would be a resolution to his problem at school.

## Claire

Running away from home was second nature to Claire. After the first time she spent a night away from home — in the company of a fairground operator — it seemed like an easy thing to do. Rather than deciding that once was enough, she decided it was fun.

Claire, who was only eleven on that first occasion, ran away seven times in as many years. It must be said that she was a rather permissive young lady and that was often at the root of her disappearances. It was only a few weeks after she first ran off that she tried it again. This time she was discovered staying with another family who had taken her in.

When she was at home, she was frequently absent from school, she had no interest in lessons, and she refused to apply herself to anything she disliked doing. It was only a matter of time before her misdemeanours came to the notice of the social services. They tried to deal with her problems in a number of ways, but they all failed to help. Finally, they took her into care.

Even then she kept escaping, and the authorities moved her from home to home, each stricter and more secure than the last. She ended up behind lock and key. It seemed that this was the only way to stop this habitual runner from continuing her wayward behaviour.

But Claire was undaunted. She bided her time until she was presented with another opportunity to escape. She was confident that the chance would arise — and it did, in the unlikely guise of a visit from the Queen Mother. Plans for the royal visit were made well in advance. Everything was scrubbed and washed — the walls and paintwork positively gleamed. Carpets were hoovered and hoovered again, pictures were hung and straightened and windows were polished as if they were precious diamonds preparing to go on display in Hatton Garden.

The authorities who ran the home felt that when the Queen Mother arrived at the building, she ought to be allowed easy access to all the rooms. Rather than going through the palaver of unlocking and locking doors, which, they thought, would not look good, they would unlock all the doors for the duration of the visit.

Claire was quick to take advantage of this temporary 'open doors' policy. She and another girl escaped during the day and spent several days living rough before they were found. During this particular spell of freedom, the two girls were offered shelter from the rain in a Panda car, by a policeman who obviously had no idea he was harbouring runaways. When the rain eased off, he told the girls he had to go, so they would have to get out. Little did he know how Claire and her friend laughed over the incident.

On another occasion, Claire became ill while on the run. She checked in at a local hospital's casualty department, and although she had no doctor's referral, and gave a false name and address, she was treated for appendicitis.

During a series of casual sexual relationships Claire

became pregnant. She wanted to keep the child but was not interested in marrying the father — if indeed she knew who that was. By now she was deemed old enough by the law to be responsible to run her own life, and sure enough, she began to settle down and live a more normal life. There was no regular man on the scene, and Claire asserted that her series of sexual encounters had left her with no desire to have a man in her life.

What kind of effect did all this have on her family? It left Claire's mother with an inbuilt hatred for the social services.

'I'd called them in, in the first place, because I needed help and so did Claire. But they didn't solve the problem or help really as all they did was take my daughter away from me.'

Claire's parents were both amazed to find out that their daughter had no idea of the worry she had caused by her habitual running. During her many absences, they had no idea where she had gone, and Claire's mother in particular was always afraid that her daughter had been murdered and was lying, undiscovered, in some ditch or field. She now says that it seems to her that Claire had an adult's mind in a child's body, with a wanderlust spirit — and that's why she was always running.

## Susha

Other cases, no less heartbreaking for those involved, arise out of the cultural barriers faced by families whose roots are outside Europe. For example, I was asked by one Sikh father to help search for his seventeen-year-old daughter who had gone missing. He wanted assistance as he said the police weren't very helpful.

I wondered what the whole story was, and decided I

ought to at least investigate before we committed ourselves. I made the trip up to London and discovered that the police advice to the Sikh gentleman had amounted to a suggestion that he and his family should return home to their own country.

The Sikh's daughter, Susha, had shown many signs of rebellion. She had been late home from school on a number of occasions; she had wanted to go out more than her father thought was good for her; and she showed little interest in being the kind of young lady he wanted her to be. Susha's father came from a strict Pakistani background, and he believed that he could impose the same kind of restrictions on the family now that they had settled in the United Kingdom.

He was certain that Susha had gone to live with her boyfriend — something of which he definitely did not approve. He had been following the young man in question and had recruited other members of the family to help him out. Things had got to such a fever pitch that the police had warned the father off — but this only served to make him even more convinced of the validity of his crusade. He told me that when he got his hands on Susha, he would thrash the living daylights out of her. In fact, if the family had still been living in Pakistan, he said, she would have been killed by her brothers, because her boyfriend was of a different religion.

With more than a little apprehension, I decided I would, at the very least, try to find out where Susha had gone. Along with a journalist who had found out about the story, we succeeded in tracking down Susha's boyfriend, believing him to be the key to the disappearance. Although he was hostile — understandably — he invited us in. After we had talked for a while, I decided that he did indeed know where the girl was in hiding.

Before we left I gave him my telephone number in case we could help. I drove my weary way back to Devon. After an IFAC committee meeting, we decided that we couldn't really be involved any further. We felt that if we were to track down Susha we would be putting her in more danger than she was now — if indeed she was in danger. Her family, in this case, were the real threat.

These cases are only the tip of the iceberg. There are plenty of other children, coming from extremely varied social backgrounds and situations, who have run away from their home environment. There are many reasons why they do it. A look at some of the major causes reveals the complexity of the problem:

- Some children are introduced to the hard addictive drugs by drug pushers. They eventually have to leave home in search of money that will support their habit. This can not only lead to a family crisis, but destitution and, in the worst cases, death.
- Other children become hooked on glue-sniffing — an increasing problem among young teenagers. They too are in danger of being caught up in a world where death is only 'a sniff away', at the risk of being crude. We know of cases where young people who have left home become involved in all kinds of crime: theft, burglary, assault and even prostitution as a result of their habit.
- Some children fall foul, as did Susha, of their family's background and culture. Religion and race can be as dividing as they can be uniting. We have come across several cases where children have run away because of their fears that mum or dad are going to force them into something against their will.
- With rocketting divorce rates, many children find themselves in the middle of a parental split. When

mum and dad go separate ways, most children are torn inside. They want to live with mum, but don't want to lose touch with dad — or vice versa. Sometimes the pressure can be too much and the child (or children) uproots and runs to the absent parent. (Of course, the other side of the coin is that the parents themselves sometimes snatch the child from their spouse.)

New legislation in the United Kingdom is aimed at dealing with situations like this, making it much easier for the authorities to cross national and international barriers to re-unite children with the parent who has legal custody. The Church of England Children's Society has also been pressing for a seventy-two hour period which will allow time for counselling the child (and parents too!) before the child returns to the home. This could help iron out the problems that have caused the child to run away in the first place. But this idea could be used in any kind of case where parents and children have been separated, whatever the reason.

- Many other reasons can be given for why children run away. Sometimes it is a teenage romance that drives the wedge between the generations. Or it may be rules governing the styles of dress or social life, or it may be unhappiness at school. All have been known to have played a major role in driving young people away from home.

There are so many traps then, so many baits, for enticing children away from the safety and security of their homes. Drugs, authority, school, culture, divorce, family arguments and a host of other problems. Any one of these can be the catalyst that leads to worry, heartache, fear, and even danger. And that is without the ingredients of crime: kidnapping, assault, rape and murder.

# 13
# The Unsolved Disappearances

For the runaway cases, there is at least some kind of happy ending, even if it is months or a year or two later. A solution is reached which allows both children and families to get back together and to come to terms with their actions. But what of those cases which have remained unsolved for many years? Police investigations into the cases are now cold and the media spotlight is off them. But they are not just 'cases'. Each story represents a human tragedy and a family who are still deeply affected by their child's unsolved disappearance. In relating these stories, we have kept the true names of the people involved.

## David McCaig
David McCaig was just thirteen years and six months when he disappeared. He left home to go to school — but never arrived. At first, the police believed that he had run away from home of his own accord. But three days later, his bicycle was found abandoned in a deserted graveyard. In spite of this, the police continued to treat his disappearance as that of a runaway. Eventually, months later, they had to admit that they had no idea what had happened to David.

No new evidence was unearthed and David's father would still like to see a further investigation into the case. He believes that the police made a fundamental error in assuming his son had run away when there was no real evidence to support their theory. As he so rightly says, time does not cure the hurt.

## Keith Bennett

Manchester schoolboy Keith Bennett had arranged to spend the night with his grandmother. The twelve-year-old did not arrive and he has never been seen since that day in 1964. His mother is convinced that her son is dead, and lies buried somewhere on Saddleworth Moor. She thinks he may have been another victim of the notorious Moors Murderers, Ian Brady and Myra Hindley. Both are now serving sentences connected with the murder of John Kilbride and Lesley Downey.

Keith vanished at the same time that police were searching for John and Lesley. Mrs Bennett and her husband already feared for their son's life, and when the police knocked on their door one afternoon, they thought perhaps they were bringing the bad news they dreaded. Yes, they had found the body of a young boy buried on the moor. Could Mr and Mrs Bennett identify these items which were found on the body?

The personal effects were not Keith's. Some other parents would now be left the grisly task of identification. For Keith's parents, however, it meant the element of doubt remained. Was Keith alive? Or is he, even now, lying dead in an unmarked, undiscovered grave?

## April Fabb

It was the spring of 1969 when fourteen-year-old April Fabb, an East Anglian schoolgirl, pedalled off from her home in Fakenham to a neighbouring village to deliver a birthday present. The roads were isolated and well in the wilds of Norfolk. On her way, April stopped to talk to some friends. Nine minutes later she had disappeared.

The route April was taking from Fakenham was some distance from any major road, and police conducted an extensive search of the nearby lanes and fields. Some of the fields were dug over, but nothing was found that indicated what had happened to young April.

The only clue that ever emerged — and even that may have nothing to do with April's disappearance — was the discovery of a handkerchief with the initial 'A' on the corner, at a stately home in the area. All that police were left with was an abandoned bicycle and the sure knowledge that April had vanished.

Nine years after April's disappearance, the case was resurrected after similarities were noticed between the Fabb mystery and the disappearance of Genette. But nothing new transpired and even today the file remains unsolved.

So many years on, the Fabbs can't help but continue looking for April. They look, like I do, in passing cars, fields, shopping centres and anywhere that might possibly be *the* place. But like many others, as they look around the country they have been impressed with the enormity of the task. How can anyone find anyone when there are so many places to look?

## Stephen Newing

Young Stephen Newing was only eleven years old when he disappeared one afternoon. He'd been out playing with his friends and had promised his mother that he would be home for tea. But Stephen never returned. The only clue he left to ever suggest he had been playing that afternoon, was his abandoned satchel.

Stephen's parents were divorced and it was thought that perhaps he had gone to see his father. But that line of investigation drew a blank. That was in 1969 — and he hasn't been heard of since.

Mrs Newing was sure, almost from the very start of her son's disappearance, that Stephen was dead. She had buried him in her mind, but because his body had never been found, she was unable to bury him in her heart. She was one of many parents whose grief will last until the riddle is solved — or until death overtakes them. Without a funeral there is no tying up of ends, no closing the chapter and starting afresh.

She had never been happy about the way the press handled the case and she wasn't happy about the police operations either. There had been some talk that Stephen had fallen down a well, but the police showed a lack of willingness to dig the well to check.

That was how IFAC got involved in its first real project. I had had some contact with Mrs Newing and went to pay her a visit. Back home again, I made some phone calls to the police on her behalf. Was it possible that Stephen had fallen down the well?

I also spoke to Mrs Newing's MP who, until this point, had done nothing to help the family in their torment. I left a message for him, and surprisingly he called me back almost immediately. He agreed to go to see Mrs Newing and to offer what help he felt he could. In spite of his previous inactivity, he went around to the Newing's home the following day. As he had promised, he made strenuous efforts to find out what really was happening.

The police told him that it was true that on his way home from playing with his friends, Stephen could have chosen a route home that would have taken him across a building site and timber yard where there was indeed a well. Although the site had been built on, it was thought that the well had not been properly capped. There were rumours that it was this well that

Stephen had fallen down. But as the police explained, rumour was indeed all it was. It had begun as one man's theory regarding Stephen's disappearance, which was overheard in a pub. As is often the way with idle chatter, the suggestion that Stephen had fallen in a well took on far more credence than it ever deserved.

It was true that there had been a well, and it was also true that it had not been properly capped. But the well was now in the back garden of a private house where it had caused a continual subsidence problem. The owner of the house had been systematically filling the well with earth to counterbalance the effects of the subsidence.

At first, I tried to encourage local firms to sponser a search of the well, but I received no response. But when I learned about the rumour and its source I decided it was a pointless exercise. At last Mrs Newing's mind was at rest and she was no longer constantly wondering if that well had been Stephen's final resting place.

Although Stephen had lived in the same area as April Fabb, the girl from Fakenham who had disappeared, the police stated that there was no link between the two cases. How they could be so sure when there had been next to no clues about either case, I don't know.

# 14
# How Can We Help?

Every hour in Britain at least two children go missing. Some have run away over a family row. Some just forget to tell mum and dad where they are going. Others run away from broken homes, broken relationships, broken lives. A percentage are bored with the routine of an ordinary life and are lured away from their homes in search of the excitement they feel they lack.

But others — they have no say in their sudden disappearance. They are the ones that become one more crime statistic — the victims of murder, kidnap, rape or assault. For some, there is a light at the end of the tunnel and they are rescued. For others the only end is death. And before death, there is pain, distress and fear.

Most of these children have parents for whom their disappearance, however short-lived, signals the blackest nightmare. Every parent suffers it to a degree, when their son or daughter stays out playing with friends for five minutes longer than they should. Or for an agonizing twenty minutes or so in that large department store when junior has disappeared. It is times like that when your heart really starts to thump and fears begin to flash through your mind.

Magnify that short-lived concern a hundred-fold and you begin to have some idea of the hell parents whose children truly *have* vanished, go through.

Although this book concerns itself mainly with under eighteen-year-olds who have disappeared, it is worth remembering that not only the young go missing. The Salvation Army receives reports of about 5,000 people each year in the United Kingdom, who leave (or are forced to leave) home. These people are all over the age of seventeen, and they are nowhere near the total number of people in this age group who go missing. They are just the cases that the Salvation Army agrees to accept. In the 17-25 age bracket, slightly more men than women are reported — in total representing 12 per cent of all the Army's inquiries. The average age of all the people on their books is 39.9. All of these disappearances cause distress, uncertainty, and often hardship.

Coupled with this, a frightening 14,000 or so British children under the age of eighteen are reported missing from their home in any one year. Although many of them are found or return of their own accord, many others don't. By the end of 1983, 727 children were known to have been missing for over a year. Children like these and their families are the main concern of IFAC.

International Find a Child is a charity, and has three aims. Firstly, we seek to give comfort, assistance and moral support to the parents of missing children. Secondly, we try to lighten the load of parents with missing children by arranging press conferences and interviews for them, and acting on their behalf, if they are willing. Thirdly, we are committed to form an international network of organizations and individuals who are concerned for missing children. We also work to suggest measures to strengthen the chances of finding missing children. We would like to see new attitudes to this serious problem adopted by both police and parliament. And we also speak in schools, talking to children and parents about what they can do to stay out of danger.

There is a lot of mileage to be gained from preventative measures, and this is why I visit schools to talk to children about the importance of not talking to strangers or accepting sweets or lifts in cars. We have found that children are more responsive when they hear someone like me talking to them because they know that my own daughter has gone missing. It seems to have more impact on them.

But we believe that the main job of educating children to avoid danger has to be done by the parents themselves. Many parents who are in touch with us say they have found it helpful to explain to their children exactly what a 'stranger' is. A stranger is anyone who is not normally welcomed into the home. Strangers include the milkman, meter readers, insurance salesmen, and the other regular callers at a child's home. The only people who are not strangers are the family and close friends.

So how should a child react to a stranger? When an unknown adult rolls down the window of his car and asks the way, what should a child do? We used to advise children in this type of situation to say, 'I'm not allowed to talk to you,' and then walk away. But we now feel that by the time a child has said this, he or she could quite easily have been snatched. It is better for them to appear rude by ignoring the stranger and walking away rather than to put themselves at risk. This may seem rude and impolite, but think about it. No adult should ever be so thoughtless as to ask children he does not know for directions. It encourages children to talk to strangers — something you would never allow *your* child to do.

Another way of minimizing the dangers is for

parents to *always* know where their child is. Parents should always discuss with children where they are going and at exactly what time they will be back home. But it is important that children should not see all these precautions as a way of keeping them under lock and key. The child needs to know that parents do this not to discipline them, or to make their life a misery, but because they love them. Children who understand this appreciate the concern, and can become very cooperative.

Keeping in touch while out is another important way of staying safe. Very young children should be taught their telephone number before their address — it is much easier to learn and means that parents of a found child can be contacted straight away. We know some families who make a game of this by turning the phone number into a song to make it fun to learn. Older children should be taught how to make a reverse charge call as soon as they can. It may one day be a lifeline if they are stranded without money.

We have also stressed to children in schools the importance of letting their parents know of any changes in plan that will make them late. 'Mum, I'm going to be late, I've missed the bus.' 'Dad, I'd like to stay out an hour longer — is that okay?' Doing this is far safer than not letting parents know.

And if children ever do get lost, they should be taught what to do. They should always look for a policeman or woman to ask for help — and if there isn't one around, then ask a lady. Some parents take the trouble of pinning their name, address and phone number in their children's coat pockets in the case of young children. The child can then use this in getting help.

In cases where children do go missing, the preventative measures give way to casualty treatment. International Find a Child can offer emotional and practical support to the suffering parents. As well as providing a listening ear and a shoulder to cry on, we are able to organize the printing of leaflets, car stickers and newsletters. We can help to arrange media coverage and advise the parents on the do's and don'ts of publicity. We are also available to say the things that the family cannot yet say, and to ask the police about the investigation.

But we also want to encourage parents to help themselves. We don't arrive on their doorstep with the intention of doing everything for them — taking the situation out of their hands. We don't want them to feel utterly helpless. Instead, we show them that they are in a position to do something positive. It is important for the parents to take a real interest in any investigations and in what is happening around them. Even if it's making a few phone calls, delivering a few posters or leaflets in the area — or sharing experiences with other parents — it's much better than sitting around doing nothing.

And parents can take the initiative with the police. If a parent is sure that their child has not run away of his or her own accord then they should continually contact the police and insist that they look at the case in a different light. Persistence pays off!

The other people who can help are, of course, friends and neighbours. The first reaction of most people when a neighbour's child goes missing is to shy away from them. And yet local friends and neighbours are ideally placed — on the spot — to help the stricken family in many, many ways.

A call simply to say 'I'm sorry' makes a world of difference. Parents in this kind of situation forget that they have stomachs that need regular meals. Cooking a meal in your own home and taking it around is a practical way of showing that you do care. Parents of lost children also lose confidence — they can't face going out, and shopping becomes a major ordeal. A good neighbour can call in the morning and offer to do the shopping, look after the other kids, help with the search — anything that shows that the parents are not alone.

People often feel that they are useless — they can do nothing to really help the parents. And yet even the smallest act of kindness can do great things. And if you are prepared to listen, to lend an ear to anything they want to pour out, then you are going to be of great value. Leave a phone number. Tell them that they can call at any hour of the day or night. What matters is not necessarily what you say, but simply being there.

Quite apart from the day-to-day practicalities of helping parents in distress, what measures need to be taken by society at large to reduce the size of the problem? International Find a Child is campaigning at present on three fronts to make the task of finding missing children easier.

Firstly, we want to see the formation of one single police agency in the United Kingdom to specialize in the problem of lost children for the whole country. At present, each force conducts its own investigation, and some are better at doing this than others.

We believe that just as there is a Drugs Squad, there should also be a Missing Persons Squad. This would also mean that full, up-to-date and accurate statistics would be kept to see the size of the problem.

In the Marie Payne case, the murder was committed in the Metropolitan police area, but the murderer, Colin Evans, lived in Reading, in the Thames Valley police area. The magazine *Police Review* criticized the Thames Valley police for failing to pass on information about Colin Evans after they had been asked to do this by the Metropolitan police. This breakdown in communication is typical of the present system and shows the urgent need for a single squad to specialize in this vitally important area.

Secondly, IFAC is campaigning for all United Kingdom schools to photograph their pupils once a year, and to keep the current photograph in their school files. At present, school photographs are bought only by parents and the school itself keeps no record. A photograph taken each year would mean that the police could be given an up-to-date photo for publicity and posters. This was something that had not happened in Genette's case. The photo that was used for most of the publicity surrounding her disappearance was quite old, and it didn't really give a good indication of what this growing-up schoolgirl was like.

Schools in Devon and Cornwall have now started to follow this scheme. Part of our campaign has been to ask the companies who come to schools to do the photography if they would donate one small photograph of each pupil to the school for their records. Many companies are willing to do this, if the schools are interested.

Thirdly, we are trying to persuade parents to fingerprint their children — something that can again help the police enormously if a child goes missing. Compulsory fingerprinting smacks too much of criminal records, but an idea from the United States holds a lot of promise. The idea is that a company sponsors the printing of cards which parents can use to fill in details of their children's height, weight, their fingerprints, and to attach a small photograph. The card is then kept, like any family papers, by the parents. It is only given to the police in the dreadful event that a child goes missing. These identity cards would be made available at the paying-in point of supermarkets and local shops.

All these are ways that we believe can help to speed the work of the police. We, and many of our supporters, are convinced that there is still plenty to be done if investigations into cases of disappeared children are to be as effective as they need to be.

When we first floated the idea of International Find a Child, back in 1978, we seemed to catch people's imagination. Soon after our idea became news we were interviewed on television, radio, and even on the Jimmy Young show. Even then the statistics were terrifying — one report said that in 1977, 14,000 children went missing from their homes. A large number of these either returned home of their own accord or were found within one or two days, but the statistics made us realize the magnitude of the problem.

It has taken much longer than we ever thought possible for us to start operating in an effective, organized way. It is incredible to me to see that out of the agony and despair of Genette's disappearance, so many good things have grown. If someone had said to me back in 1978, when Ginny first went missing, that good could and would come out of it, I don't know what I would have done. Felt like hitting him very hard, I think.

But now as I look back, I can see how one thing led to another, bringing me slowly but surely to a new acceptance of myself. I can't express the relief it is to know that God loves me just as I am, and that I don't have to prove myself anymore.

And I can see now why God did not allow IFAC to take off in the early days after Genette disappeared. He knew that a confused and embittered leadership would only lead others further into the dark. Not that he has finished work on me yet! I am a long way off perfect. And I think it is true that I don't yet know Genette's ultimate fate because if I did, IFAC would stop dead. The time for me to find out about Genette won't come until the organization stands strong on its own two feet, whether I am there or not. And that time has not yet come.

So I'll just have to be patient.

Not a day goes by when I don't think about Genette, or wonder just a little about her fate. But now, those memories aren't confused with feelings of bitterness and hatred; with thoughts of violence and destruction. It's not like that anymore.

Thank God.

# Useful Addresses

**International Find a Child**
Freepost
Okehampton EX20 1YZ
Telephone: 0837 4335
(Donations can be sent to International Find a Child c/o Trustee Savings Bank plc, Okehampton, Devon.)

**C.A.R.E. Trust**
21A Down Street
London W1Y 7DN
Telephone: 01-409 0111
(Will put you in touch with the Christians in your locality who are willing to help.)

**Salvation Army**
Missing Persons Bureau
110 Middlesex Street
London E1
Telephone: 01-247 6831
(Undertakes the tracing of missing relatives for the purpose of reconciliation only. There are also local branches.)

**Message Home**
Telephone: 01-799 7662 or 021 426 3396
(A confidential service run by the Mothers' Union to help runaways contact their parents. No need to say where you are. Just dial, say who the message is for, and give your message.)

**Missing Children Help Center**
410 Ware Boulevard
Suite 1102
Tampa
Florida
USA
Telephone: 010 1 813 623 5437